POWER OF 2

**HOW TO MAKE
THE MOST OF YOUR
PARTNERSHIPS AT WORK
AND IN LIFE**

RODD WAGNER AND
GALE MULLER, PH.D.

GALLUP PRESS
1251 Avenue of the Americas
23rd Floor
New York, NY 10020

ISBN: 978-1-59562-029-3
Library of Congress Control Number: 2009930989

First Printing: 2009
10 9 8 7 6 5 4 3 2 1

To Nora
- RGW

To Kay
- GDM

Table of Contents

**

Introduction

Made for Collaborating

Face it. Your partnerships could use some help.

If you are like most people, you've had some good ones. You may even have a few of them now. Yet chances are you don't make the most of the collaborative opportunities all around you. You are surrounded by potential partners: colleagues, neighbors, friends, fellow volunteers. You know many people, and they know you. But powerful partnerships — the kind in which you and a collaborator regularly work together, reach goals together you never could have accomplished apart, and gain the deep satisfaction only such an alliance can bring — are elusive.

You almost certainly spend much of your time working on projects for which you alone are responsible, feeling the full pressure of having to do the whole thing yourself, even the aspects that are not your strength. And when, somehow, you struggle through and complete the job, you turn it in, perhaps get a little recognition from your boss, and move on to the next requirement, which you will also do largely by yourself.

You are not alone in having this problem. Somewhere we got off track. Somehow our televisions, e-mail, headphones, cell phones, car radios, and personal computers trick our brains into thinking we are with other people, interacting, when we are, in fact, working in isolation. We are crowded in offices, airports, subways — frequently within arm's reach of dozens of people — but often on a very lonely pursuit. Wired? Yes. Networked? Yes. Collaborating? Not much.

Humans are made for collaborating. We like music because the songs of our deepest ancestors helped them work together. Our blood pressure rises and falls depending on who is nearby. The amount we eat depends a lot on the amount eaten by those with whom we dine. We laugh, not so much because something is funny, but because laughter is a kind of social glue; a person is 30 times more likely to laugh when he's with somebody than when he is alone.

When you watch someone, a network of "mirror neurons" in your brain rehearses what he is doing, giving you the ability to see things from his perspective. If one person in a conversation uses a certain word — calls an object's color *turquoise*, for example — the other person will probably use the same word rather than a synonym such as *teal*. We unconsciously adjust our grammar and word choices to match what the other person already said. It's a subconscious way of signaling "I agree with you." This mimicry, one study found, "is automatic and reflects the fact that humans are designed for dialogue rather than monologue."

Having a collaborator changes our perception of reality. Volunteers in one experiment were asked to estimate the weight of a basket of potatoes before they touched it. Those who were told they would have help lifting the basket gave lower weight estimates than those who were told they would have to lift it by themselves. "We plan our actions guided partly by what we think we can achieve with others," wrote one of the researchers who conducted the basket experiment.

In a world that emphasizes individual achievement — the successful CEO, the MVP, the star — we often forget that everyone is descended from millions of people who survived because they didn't go it alone. In the thousands of years that molded human nature, our ancestors required not only individual wits and strength, but also the ability to collaborate — to discern, trust, sacrifice, empathize, and intelligently combine their efforts with someone else. "The evolution of human beings has consisted largely of adaptation to one another," wrote one commentator. Hunters who worked together were more likely to return with a kill. Two men who agreed to help each other improved their odds of fending off mutual enemies.

Yet over time, humans created so many conveniences that we now can survive without each other. We live indoors rather than in the elements. We can eat microwavable dinners instead of hauling in a fish net with someone else. We no longer tell real stories around the fire; we turn on the TV and watch familiar strangers pretend.

Cubicles and private offices were bad enough; at least we would pass each other in the hall or gather for lunch. Now we can telecommute, staying in our home offices and e-mailing the work we did by ourselves. One hiring manager complained the job candidates she sees are "so used to texting, they don't even know how to carry on a basic conversation with other people." We are collaborative creatures in a newly do-it-yourself world.

Isolation is bad for you. It poses dangers as serious as cigarette smoking, high blood pressure, high cholesterol, obesity, or lack of exercise, one research summary concluded. Conversely, the more good partnerships you have in your life, the more likely you are to say that you experienced the feeling of enjoyment much of the day yesterday, that you recently learned something interesting, and that you've been doing a lot of smiling and laughing — all key measures of your happiness. Even having one strong partnership markedly increases your well-being over those who have none.

In the workplace, employees with just one collaborative relationship are 29 percent more likely to say they will stay with their company for the next year and 42 percent more likely to intend to remain with their current employer for their entire career, compared to those with no partnerships. Those who feel well-teamed with one or more colleagues are substantially more engaged at work. They generate higher customer scores and better safety, retention, creativity, productivity, and profitability for the business — and a greater level of happiness for themselves.

For all of our collaborative instincts, most of us today form far fewer strong partnerships than we could, or than we should. Gallup's research reveals that the median number of work partnerships for an American employee is just four, but even that number hides a more troubling truth. The small proportion of people who have dozens of close teammates inflates the statistic. When asked how many strong alliances they have, most people say they have just a few, even though the highest levels of happiness and employee engagement kick in when a person has 5 to 10 good alliances.

The most disturbing statistic is that the most common number of work partnerships — the answer given by 16 percent of the population — is zero. Asked if they have *ever* had a great partnership at work, nearly one-quarter of employees say no.

"The sad thing is that I've never had a successful partnership," one businessperson told us. "I've been thrown into the leadership role in every single 'group project' or organized group outside or inside of school. Every time, I've become the leader, ended up doing the majority of the work, and gotten the majority of the credit. I've learned — again sadly — that I'm better at taking care of my responsibilities myself and not depending on others for creative success in my personal, artistic, or professional futures."

"In thinking through my best and worst work partnerships," said one manager at a medical device manufacturer, "I keep seeing more experiences in the 'worst' column and a sparsely populated 'best' section."

At the highest corporate levels, flying solo can have consequences for all the employees and shareholders. As the two of us began circulating Gallup's partnership discoveries inside some of the world's most prominent companies, we were surprised at how readily an acrimonious relationship at the top came to mind among those who have to tiptoe around the landmines.

"Grace and Randy hate each other," said one midlevel executive. "They say all the right things in meetings, but that's just for show. They have separate empires. You're either on Grace's team or on Randy's team." Whether the rift is between the chief operating officer and the chief financial officer or between the top marketing executive and the head of sales, such failures to collaborate are seldom private, nor are they trivial for the rest of the organization. Companies that should be concentrating on the battle with the competition are instead consuming their resources waging elaborate civil wars between the camps of Executive A and Executive B.

Equally troublesome is the concentration of power in the hands of a lone leader whose human foibles cannot help but be magnified under the pressure of having to be too many things to too many people. "America's most serious corporate governance problem is the Imperial CEO — a leader who is both chairman of the company's board of directors as well as its chief executive officer," wrote former Northwest Airlines Chairman Gary Wilson, who served on the boards of Yahoo! and Disney. "Such a CEO can dominate his board and is accountable to no one." Companies need, he argued, not one at the top, but two.

Seeing these patterns at numerous client companies, the two of us teamed up to lead what became a five-year endeavor to crack the code on collaboration, to discover what elements are crucial for two people becoming a successful team. We found the answers in some fascinating areas: in research showing how monkeys react when working in pairs, in a computerized friend-or-foe contest that baffled the experts, in studies of revenge, and in "irrational" acts of self-sacrifice.

We also launched waves of original Gallup research to identify the dimensions of partnership and to determine how to best measure them. We analyzed the responses of thousands of people in search of the variables that are best at differentiating between a great partnership and a poor one. People from all walks of life scored their working relationships with their coworkers, fellow volunteers, other students, managers, and hundreds of others with whom they regularly interact. As we studied the stories of successful partners, famous and obscure, these aspects came into stark relief.

Throughout your life, you have opportunities to build hundreds of partnerships. Some are brief relationships to accomplish a modest goal. Others last years, even decades. These opportunities and relationships are often poorly understood and frequently mismanaged.

Why do some people click and others clash? Why do some people have dozens of great partnerships while others have none? Great partnerships don't just happen. Whether your joint mission is to build a successful company, coach a team, improve the government, do something spectacular for a charity, or any other worthy goal, all successful partnerships share the same crucial ingredients. Although the answers to what makes a great collaboration were scattered across many sources and scientific disciplines, when combined, they make a cohesive set of insights you can use to make the most of your partnerships at work and in your personal life.

The research revealed eight elements of a powerful partnership:

Complementary Strengths: Everyone has weaknesses and blind spots that create obstacles to reaching a goal. One of the most powerful reasons for teaming up is working with someone who is strong where you are weak, and vice versa. Specialization allows both people to spend more time doing what each does best and allows the two to tackle together challenges neither could alone. Individuals are not well-rounded, but pairs can be.

A Common Mission: It may seem as if the pursuit of a shared goal is so basic to a collaboration that it goes without saying. Yet when a partnership fails, the root cause is often that the two people were pursuing separate agendas. Conversely, when partners want the same thing badly enough, they will make the personal sacrifices necessary to see it through.

Fairness: Humans have an instinctive need for fairness. It appears very early in childhood without any training. No one likes to be taken advantage of, to get the short end of the deal. Because the need for fairness runs deep, it is an essential quality of a strong partnership.

Trust: Working with someone means taking risks. You are not likely to contribute your best work unless you trust that your partner will do her best. You need to rely on your counterpart to look out for your interests. She requires the same from you. Without trust, it's easier to work alone.

Acceptance: We see the world through our own set of lenses. What's normal for one person is a serious flaw for another. Whenever two disparate personalities come together, there is bound to be a certain friction from their differences. This can be a recipe for conflict unless both learn to accept the idiosyncrasies of the other.

Forgiveness: People are imperfect. They make mistakes. They sometimes do the wrong thing. Without forgiveness, the natural revenge motives that stem from friend-or-foe instincts will overpower all the reasons to continue a partnership, and it will dissolve.

Communicating: The only way two minds can be united in one mission is if the pair communicates well. Without coordinating their moves, collaborators risk knocking heads or making deal-wrecking assumptions about the other's intentions. In the early stages of a partnership, communicating helps to prevent misunderstandings and to assure each person of the other's trustworthiness. Later in the relationship, a continuous flow of information makes the work more efficient by keeping the two people synchronized.

Unselfishness: Many people enter partnerships for selfish reasons; they can accomplish more collaborating than they can working solo. However, in the best working relationships, something happens along the way. Some researchers call it "mutuality" when the natural concern for your own welfare transforms into gratification in seeing your comrade succeed. Those who have reached this level say such collaborations become among the most fulfilling aspects of their lives. It is one thing to have accomplished a great goal by oneself, they say, but individual achievements cannot compare to doing a great thing together.

When all these elements combine, partnerships become not just effective in accomplishing the mission, but also personally rewarding, sometimes intensely so. "If I were teaching students about entrepreneurship, I'd point out that many of the great startups of the last 30 years began as teams of two," wrote *Forbes* Publisher Rich Karlgaard. "Behind this phenomenon is a principle: Build on your strengths. To mitigate your weaknesses — and we all have them — partner up! Find your complement."

Ultimately, if you can harness the same cooperative instincts that allowed your distant ancestors to survive, you will enjoy greater happiness. You can lighten your load, take advantage of your strengths, and achieve unprecedented success by being one of two people pursuing a shared mission. Take off the headphones. Break away from the screen. Get out of your office. And unleash the Power of 2.

Chapter One

Complementary Strengths

"The same man cannot be skilled in everything;
each has his special excellence."

— Euripides

SEVERAL DECADES AGO, a junior high shop teacher wanted to impress upon his new students the dangers of the oxyacetylene torch. "Pay attention, class," he said, pulling a balloon from his pocket and holding it to the nozzle of the torch. "I am going to fill this balloon with oxygen." When the balloon was full, he lit a match under it, producing a strong pop. "Not bad, eh?" said the teacher, smiling at the rapt students.

He pulled another balloon from his pocket. "Now this time, I am going to fill the balloon with acetylene," he said. Following the same procedure, he made a short flare as the fuel caught fire. "Wow!" said the kids. "Cool!"

The teacher pulled yet another balloon from his pocket. "You've seen what happens to each of these elements separately. Now let me show you what happens when I put them together." He repeated the procedure a third time, opening the valves for the oxygen and the acetylene as the balloon grew larger. "You might want to plug your ears," said the teacher, putting the flame to the latex.

BAM!

The mixture exploded with such force, the students could hear it loudly despite their plugged ears. Their jaws dropped as they looked at one another. Point made.

Was it the oxygen or the acetylene that caused the explosion? Neither. Or rather, both. Separately, they are impressive. Together, they create a mixture so hot it can melt steel. The power is in the combination.

Your partnerships work on the same principle. The best happen when you and someone who has strengths that complement yours join forces and focus on a single goal. Your strengths cancel out your partner's weaknesses, and vice versa. You accomplish together what could not be done separately.

Before you can forge a successful alliance, you must understand what you bring to the combination, and equally important, what you don't. Collaboration is more than doubling up — more than just twice the oxygen or twice the acetylene. The key to achieving success is not trying to be someone else or striving to be as good as your collaborator at whatever he does best or seeking to be universally proficient. It's in discovering your own exceptional abilities, recognizing your weaknesses, and understanding how someone else's abilities complement your own.

This combination of reciprocal abilities was at the heart of what we discovered during five years of research into collaboration. Through repeated waves of surveying, we asked thousands of randomly selected adults to identify a successful partnership and a failed one (outside of their family). We then asked them to respond to parallel statements about both of those relationships.

Their responses were analyzed to identify the statements that, when answered positively, best predict collaborative success (and when answered negatively, best foreshadow failure). In the end, 23 statements made the cut to become part of the Gallup Partnership Rating Scales.

Three of these statements emerged as the most important for determining how well your abilities mesh with those of your collaborator:

- We complement each other's strengths.
- We need each other to get the job done.
- He or she does some things much better than I do, and I do some things much better than he or she does.

Survey participants rated their level of agreement with each of the statements on a scale from 1 ("strongly disagree") to 5 ("strongly agree"). Ratings that averaged less than 3.0 are classified as "poor" or "very poor." These responses were typical of relationships in which the participant felt he or she could just as easily do something alone as rely on the other person. Scores of at least 3.0 but less than 3.6 are considered "borderline," the ho-hum area that, while it may lack acrimony, also lacks intensity. Averages greater than 3.6 are in the "good" range.

We were surprised how strongly a collaborator had to score all three of these statements to demonstrate that he or she was in a resilient alliance. Only by answering 5 to all three statements does a participant indicate a level of complementary strengths that Gallup considers "exceptional." Why no tolerance for less-than-perfect scores? Because the most important reference point on such a scale is not the middle, but the top. Answering 4 to any of the statements, while good in an absolute sense, also indicates a full point of reservation — something substantial that is keeping you from giving the most positive response. In practice, this holding back is costly. It reveals that you and your counterpart are not quite a perfect fit or don't absolutely need each other to get the job done. In exceptional two-person teams, there is no such reservation.

These statements reflect not just interdependence, but a mutual recognition of it. One person we interviewed told us how her creativity combined well with a colleague's attention to details. Two producers of programming for a children's medical center discovered that the understanding one had of the hospital's communication needs complemented the other's writing, editing, and video skills. Coeditors of a newsletter found that their work was effective because, as one of them said, "We each contributed something the other lacked, I a sense of style and she a specific political awareness, so that what we wrote wouldn't embarrass anyone."

The characteristics that make a partnership solid could be anything from a physical attribute (the height of a basketball forward) or a credential (a medical license) to experience in a certain field (a decade as an architect) or personal reputation (a relationship with every media buyer in the market). You should be able to name these qualities for yourself and your counterpart without much hesitation: "I bring _____ to the partnership; my partner adds _____."

Anything crucial to accomplishing the goal that one person lacks and the other has increases your rationale for working together. Sometimes what's required is the difference in how the two of you think or act. One consistently sees the potential; the other routinely sees the risks. One generates ideas; the other puts them into production. One is good with technology; the other is good with people.

A successful collaborator must resist the ego-gratifying temptation to take too much credit. If a person honestly recognizes that his counterpart does some things much better than he does and that he needs the other person to get the job done, he is less susceptible to fall into the trap of conceit. In a strong partnership, both participants are always promoting the abilities of the other. They constantly speak in terms of "we" or "us," rather than "I" or "me."

People often confuse collaboration with friendship, but they are not the same thing. While getting along is important to both kinds of relationships, if you team up with a buddy whose strengths do not complement your own, don't be surprised if you find yourselves being more social than successful. Some of your best potential partners are people with whom you have yet to build strong personal rapport but who nonetheless have the oxygen to go with your acetylene.

Strong partnerships prevail despite a persistent cultural bias for focusing on individual achievements. Many observers of a two-person team want to know which of them is the real reason for their success, failing to understand that neither is the complete equation.

OXYGEN AND ACETYLENE MET in Salt Lake City in 1985, when the Utah Jazz drafted Karl Malone from Louisiana Tech University, making him a teammate of point guard John Stockton. They were markedly different men who, over the next 18 years, would achieve more than any other duo in professional basketball. Yet even when their complementary abilities were on public display, they encountered the same pervasive bias that only one of them must be the secret to their shared success.

When Stockton joined Utah the year before Malone, he was third in line behind established starter Rickey Green and backup Jerry Eaves. Quiet, humble, and only 6-foot-1, Stockton was so concerned that his first year with the Jazz would be his last that he held out for an extra $5,000 of pay. He didn't make a major purchase until four months into his rookie season, when he bought a TV for his one-bedroom apartment to watch the Super Bowl. His concern was misplaced. Stockton set new Jazz rookie records with 109 steals and 415 assists, despite averaging only 18 minutes per game, less than half the time he would typically play in future years.

Malone entered the professional draft at an intimidating 6-foot-9 and 256 pounds, large enough to hold his own near the basket, fast enough to beat other forwards down the court, and a solid shooter outside. He earned the nickname "Mailman" in college because, it was said, he always delivered. For all that, 12 teams passed him over before the Jazz selected him in the first round of the draft.

As a higher profile acquisition and a bigger player than Stockton, Malone got more chances to shine as a rookie, averaging almost 31 minutes per game. The early reviews were good. In his first season, he put the ball through the hoop once every four minutes and six seconds he was on the court.

While Malone proved himself, Stockton improved himself. He got more playing time — over 23 minutes per game — and made better use of it. The frequency of his baskets increased from once every six-and-a-half minutes on the court to once every six minutes and eight seconds. He stole the ball from the opposing team almost twice a game, and he shaved 25 seconds off his time between assists.

As Stockton and Malone each improved their own games and earned more time on the court, they had more opportunities to work together. Four games into the 1987-1988 season, Jazz coach Frank Layden made Stockton the starter, giving him 50 percent more playing time. The stage was set for the Stockton-Malone partnership to emerge. As the accolades for both players rolled in, reporters began noticing the synergy between them.

Under Layden's strategy, the point guard had the ball much of the time, so it was not surprising that his new starter in that position was putting up good numbers. "There are two other major reasons why Stockton gets a lot of assists — Karl Malone posting up on the blocks and Karl Malone steaming down court on the fast break. An assist man needs a 'finisher,'" wrote Jack McCallum in a 1988 *Sports Illustrated* article, "and it's no secret that Stockton is looking for the 'Mailman' most of the time."

A chemistry, mutual respect, and at times eerie coordination formed between the two men. Equally obsessed with winning, they worked tirelessly and found a rhythm together. "I've never seen Karl tired," said Stockton. "He's on a different level than the rest of us." They developed a personal bond that was greater than their interdependence on the court. "What John Stockton doesn't know is that he is like one of my older brothers to me, and not because he gives me the ball on the break," said Malone. "Mess with Stockton, and you mess with me."

They formed their alliance even though, in many respects, they were opposites. Malone constantly talked about himself, often in the third person. "The best thing that could have happened to Karl Malone," said Malone, "was coming to Salt Lake City." His public quarrels with Jazz owner Larry Miller became a mainstay of local news reports.

Stockton, on the other hand, not only avoided self-analysis, he didn't even like talking about himself in response to direct questions from reporters. "You talk about yourself and it's such an individual-sounding thing," he told one sportswriter. "To me, it's offensive. I'm just not comfortable with it. I guess if I played an individual sport like tennis or something, I'd be out of a job. I just don't think in terms of 'I did this' or 'I did that.'"

Malone drove a shiny Harley-Davidson motorcycle and wore a leather fringe jacket and cowboy boots. He bought a semitrailer and had it painted with what one writer called "a striking Western mural that suggests Frederic Remington on an acid trip." The lead cowboy in the mural was Malone himself.

Stockton drove a Chevy Suburban and wore golf shirts, khakis, and white sneakers. When he got married, he made sure the announcement in his hometown newspaper said only that the groom was "employed in Salt Lake City." He called his life away from basketball "pretty boring," seeking to dissuade public interest in his life as much as Malone welcomed the attention.

But it was their complementary differences on the court that put them in the record books. Stockton played the role of "field general," setting up the play. Malone's talent was executing in the key. "To my eye, it seemed like the real glue that held the relationship together was the understanding of how much each one needed the other," said Michael C. Lewis, a *Salt Lake Tribune* sports reporter who wrote a book about the team. "There was a real full understanding on each of their parts that where they were trying to go, which was to win an NBA championship, neither one of them was going to get there without the other."

As it became increasingly successful on the court, the partnership flummoxed the statisticians and observers. Sportswriters insisted on trying to isolate one man's performance from the other. The rhythm between Malone and Stockton really threw them.

"As long as Stockton is around, Malone will never get full credit for being a great player. The question of who's more important — Malone or Stockton, scorer or passer — is a chicken-or-egg conundrum that simply can't be solved. And the more success they have as a tandem, the more complex the question becomes," wrote *Sports Illustrated*. "Neither Malone nor Stockton will become the MVP as long as they play together: They cancel each other out."

Nothing exemplifies the coordination between the two players better than what happened in Game 4 of the 1997 NBA Finals. After being down 71-66 to the Chicago Bulls, Stockton nearly evened the score with a three-pointer and three free throws matched by just one basket from the Bulls.

The Jazz were losing 72 to 73 with only a minute remaining. Bulls guard Michael Jordan took a shot and missed. Stockton, who had sneaked up to the basket, got the rebound. He turned and fired the ball down the court, where Malone was racing just ahead of Jordan. It was an extremely risky play. "If you could have suspended time right then, when the ball was in the air, [Jazz coach] Jerry [Sloan] probably would have strangled me," said Stockton. "I saw Karl had position, and when he does, he's the best at getting the ball."

Malone had similar faith in his teammate. "I knew Michael was back there, lurking, but I also knew that if anybody could get the pass to me, it was Stock," said the forward. "When he threw it, I thought, 'Well, Stock doesn't throw bad passes, so I must be open.'" The ball landed in Malone's hands, and he made a layup to put Utah in the lead for good. The play was so improbable that sportswriters dubbed it simply "The Pass." The next morning's *Salt Lake Tribune* reported that the capacity home-arena crowd "probably still doesn't believe what it saw."

The Utah Jazz never won the NBA championship with Malone and Stockton. They came excruciatingly close in 1997 and 1998, a major accomplishment for the team from the league's smallest market. The prediction that neither man would win the MVP title was just plain wrong. Malone would go on to win it twice, not in spite of his partnership with Stockton, but because of it. The men were co-MVPs of the 1993 All-Star Game. Stockton was elected to the Basketball Hall of Fame in 2009, his first year of eligibility, almost certain to be followed by Malone.

Malone became the second-leading scorer in the NBA. Stockton became the all-time leader in assists and steals. On any list of the best who have played professional basketball, you will find the names of Stockton and Malone.

Did they cancel each other out?

Hardly.

A PERNICIOUS IDEA works its way through classrooms, into corporate training departments, and even around the dinner table in many homes. There's a good chance it hampers your working relationships. It goes by various names: the well-rounded person, the Renaissance man, *homo universalis*, or the polymath (from the Greek word *polymathēs*, meaning "having learned much"). It is the belief that anyone can accomplish anything alone with enough determination and perseverance.

Blame Leonardo da Vinci. His gifts for drawing and painting, his understanding of anatomy, and his penchant for inventing labeled him a universal genius and led millions to wonder why they had not done such remarkable things. Blame Thomas Jefferson, whose interests ranged from politics to science to architecture to agriculture. Or blame the creators of heroes such as Spider-Man, MacGyver, and James Bond — characters who appeal to us because they are self-sufficient in any crisis. We want to be like that.

This fallacy has tremendous traction in the popular press. Self-help gurus such as Tony Robbins chide their followers for hiding behind "excuses." "Using the power of decision gives you the capacity to get past any excuse to change any and every part of your life *in an instant,*" Robbins wrote in his bestseller *Awaken the Giant Within.* "If you truly decide to," he wrote in bold type, "you can do almost anything."

One book purports to help the reader learn "how to think like Leonardo da Vinci." Another book by the same author promises to teach a person how to "innovate like Edison." "Genius is made, not born. And human beings are gifted with an almost unlimited potential," proclaims the back cover of the da Vinci book.

Few ideas so widely accepted are so demonstrably wrong. The polymath is a myth. It contradicts reason, the latest research on genetic inheritance, human nature, and even the Bible (which speaks of "diversities of gifts" among different people). Da Vinci was an incredible artist and thinker, but he often struggled to finish his work. For all his talents, Jefferson was horrible at handling money, dying deeply in debt. He seemed organically incapable of the kinds of constructive confrontations that were welcomed by his sometime collaborator John Adams. And fictional characters such as James Bond are just that — fiction.

Steve Martin could stake a claim on being a Renaissance man. In addition to being a comedian, he is an actor, bestselling author, playwright, screenwriter — and an accomplished banjo player who performed several times on the *Late Show with David Letterman*. During one of those appearances, the host asked, "Do you play other instruments besides the banjo?"

"No," he told Letterman. "But, let me ask you a question: If Yo-Yo Ma were sitting here, would you say, 'You play anything else besides the cello?'"

The pressure to be all things to all people is pervasive. But doing just a few things exceptionally well is a better path to success than spreading yourself thinly across dozens of disciplines, becoming, as they say in Spanish, *aprendiz de todo, maestro de nada* (apprentice of everything, master of nothing).

When people are asked to rate themselves, researchers often find what they call the "Lake Wobegon effect," nearly everyone believing that they are above average on just about everything. A majority of Swedish drivers think they drive better than average. Most undergraduates believe they have above-average popularity. People scoring in the bottom 25 percent on tests of humor, of grammar, and of logic grossly overestimate their test performance and ability.

The flip side of this phenomenon is that people who excel at a task often think their work is unexceptional. They take for granted what comes naturally to them, assuming that others can perform the task just as well. Their overestimation of others' abilities leads them to suffer what one study called "undue modesty" about their own strengths.

As a consequence of these misconceptions, most people see themselves as more well-rounded than they really are, above average where they are weak, and close to average where they are incredible. But they're wrong. Instead of complete circles, people are puzzle pieces. Some aspects of their aptitude dramatically exceed those of the general population, while other qualities are well below the mean.

Great partners know where they are strong and where they are weak. Pierre Omidyar, founder of eBay, discovered the "analytic powerhouse" he needed for the business in Stanford MBA Jeff Skoll. "It was the perfect balance," Omidyar said of his work with Skoll. "I tended to think more intuitively, and he could say, 'Okay, let's see how we can actually get that done.'" Skoll was intensely ambitious, which helped with running the business; Omidyar was more laid-back, which helped him work with the growing group of buyers and sellers.

Legendary investor Warren Buffett realized his enthusiasm was well-tempered by Charlie Munger's skepticism. Buffett dubbed his collaborator the "abominable no-man" and claimed that together, they made better investment decisions.

The same pattern emerges in common working relationships. "I was in a retail business with another woman for about 15 years," one woman told Gallup. "She was a born leader, and I didn't mind because I am more reticent. We both made decisions together and did the work together. She had previous retail experience and helped me to grow more confident in that area, buying at market, merchandising, etc. I had always worked in an office previously and had more patience and did the checkbook. We worked well together because we were different."

So admit it: You stink at some things. You have blind spots, weaknesses, areas in which others seem to perform effortlessly while you struggle just to be average. You are also overly modest about your strengths. What seems to be no big deal to you is difficult for others. Your strengths are stronger and your weaknesses weaker than you realize. You need help. You are also precisely the help someone else needs.

Your problem is not your "excuses." It's the fallacy that you can make the basket without an assist, that you can be Edison or da Vinci or anyone else except your talented and incomplete self, or that oxygen or acetylene alone will be anywhere near as powerful as the two combined.

★★

EVERYONE KNOWS THE NAME MICHAEL EISNER. He's an icon — the former CEO of The Walt Disney Company who discovered untapped reserves of profitability in the Disney brand, made obscenely large sums of money, and then was driven from leadership when things went sour. Many books and articles have been written about him.

Yet frequently overlooked is the fact that Eisner's greatest accomplishments were not his alone, while some of his greatest failures were. Eisner's story is perhaps the greatest corporate cautionary tale about the need for a partner with complementary strengths.

Eisner was not sold to the Disney board of directors by himself. He could not have attained the position of CEO without Frank Wells, a Rhodes Scholar and former vice chairman of Warner Brothers. As the two men schemed in the early 1980s with Stanley Gold, who was Roy Disney's attorney, on how to take control of the underperforming company, it became apparent neither executive would be appointed to lead the company alone.

Eisner was president and chief operating officer of Paramount Pictures and a former senior vice president at ABC. He was considered one of the best executives in the entertainment business at finding money-making ideas. Wells, meanwhile, had a reputation for being urbane, considerate, and financially adroit.

Convincing Disney's board to hire both men was not easy. One board member interviewed Eisner and Wells on consecutive days. The former emphasized his creativity and his belief that Disney was full of new opportunities; the latter emphasized his negotiation and business skills. "But we're only looking for one CEO," said the director. "Then get Eisner," Wells said. "You need creativity more than anything else." Other board members felt Disney needed Wells more than it needed Eisner.

Eventually, in September 1984, the Disney board voted unanimously to make Eisner chairman and chief executive and to make Wells president and chief operating officer. "From that point on," wrote Eisner, "we began to sail around the world on the Disney adventure. If I was the rudder, he was the keel. For 10 years, we never had a fight or a disagreement, or even a misunderstanding."

The two men quickly established a solid working relationship in which Wells' business acumen rounded out Eisner's creative impulses. Wells concentrated on administrative and financial issues; Eisner supervised films, television projects, and Disney's theme parks. "Eisner and Wells," as one account put it, "were like right and left arms, one creative, impulsive, irreverent; the other measured, practical, decisive."

The two new Disney executives faced a daunting list of problems. Attendance at Disneyland was down 17 percent from its peak in 1980. The number of visitors to Epcot was below projections. Disney's live-action studio was not a major player. Its animated film operations were dying. Actor Tom Hanks commented that the headquarters in Burbank were like "a Greyhound bus station in the fifties." While its sources of revenue were faltering, the company lumbered forward with nearly a billion dollars in debt.

The essence of the new executives' strategy was moving money away from places where it gave little return and toward investments that might pay off. They terminated more than a thousand employees in the first year. They killed off questionable projects.

At the same time, Eisner didn't want penny pinching to stop innovation. The year after Wells and Eisner assumed control, they pumped $280 million into improving the theme parks, which was twice as much as the year before, and they increased the price of tickets. Despite the higher prices, the number of customers increased. The combined effect tripled theme park profits in three years, to $548 million in 1986.

In the search for new revenue, no issue was more controversial among executives than whether to release Disney's animated classics such as *Snow White and the Seven Dwarfs*, the company's most treasured assets, on home video. Selling the videos would tap a vast market, but it could reduce the impact of recycling the movies back to theaters every 7 to 10 years. Mass marketing could cheapen the brand.

Wells and Eisner convened a series of marathon meetings to discuss the issue. Roy Disney opposed the idea. "There are overwhelming arguments not to do this," Wells said, "but it's still important to have the debate."

Arguing such issues brought out Wells' strengths for finding the best course. "We were a remarkably complementary fit," said Eisner. "Frank was brilliant at putting all the evidence on the table, but he often found it hard to make the final decision. I never tried to come to a conclusion by logically weighing the pros and cons. Instead, with Frank's help, I kept accumulating evidence until I reached the point where a certain choice instinctively felt right." The eventual decision to release movies such as *Pinocchio, Sleeping Beauty*, and *Cinderella* successfully tapped a new vein of revenue for the company, and the home video market became a staple of the company's finances.

Wells not only helped refine the business strategy, he also kept the peace. Eisner rubbed people the wrong way. He fussed over the details of new rides. He was suspicious of others' motives, and he didn't trust many people. He had a huge ego. He needed someone to balance him. Several executives remarked that Wells kept Eisner from getting out of control. "When we had a grievance list, going to Frank was like going to the Supreme Court," said one executive. "You felt you got a fair hearing, and you felt you got justice."

"For Michael, I make life easier," Wells told *Fortune* in 1991. "For me, he makes life more fun."

From 1984 to 1994, Disney stock multiplied to more than 10 times what its value was when Eisner and Wells took the reins of the company. Both men became tremendously richer: Eisner took in $197 million in 1992 and was on the Forbes 400 list of the richest Americans. Eisner and Disney were widely criticized for the amount he was paid. Their strongest defense was that his compensation was tied directly to the growth in the company's profitability.

And then the magic ended.

During Easter weekend of 1994, Wells organized a skiing excursion in the mountains east of Elko, Nevada.

On the second day of the outing, Wells was among the passengers traveling in a helicopter when its engine flamed out and it dropped from the sky. He was killed on impact.

Eisner personally worked on the press release issued by the company. "Frank Wells has been the purest definition of a life force I have ever known," it said. "His wisdom, his charm, his zest for experience and challenge . . . his naked and awesome intelligence . . . set him apart and beyond. The world has lost a great human being."

Rather than seek a new business partner, Eisner lobbied for and received approval to assume Wells' responsibilities and titles himself. "In part, the purpose was to send an immediate signal to Wall Street and the financial community that business at Disney would continue as usual," the now Chairman-CEO-COO-president wrote in the late 1990s. "Equally important, I wanted to put to rest speculation that anyone was in line to inherit Frank's job."

After the financial success Eisner and Wells led for a decade, the Disney board apparently forgot why it installed the two of them together in 1984. Business could not "continue as usual" because Eisner was only part of the equation. If the power of their complementary abilities was not fully evident during the partnership, it was doubly apparent after the accident.

Without Wells, a book the men had planned to write together emerged instead as Eisner's vain, sanitized autobiography. It landed with a thud. "His descriptions can be so calculatingly self-serving that they lack both credibility and nuance," wrote a reviewer for *The New York Times.* "Like many celebrated chief executives, he has an ego that leaves little room for perspective."

The CEO would not create a succession plan. He refused to elevate anyone to the presidency of Disney who might show him up. Eisner repeatedly promised the number two spot to various executives, only to rebuff them when the time came to make good on his promise.

He snubbed Jeffrey Katzenberg, his colleague for nearly two decades, breaking a promise Katzenberg said Eisner made to him that if Wells' seat became vacant, the job would be his. Katzenberg's eventual lawsuit cost Disney $280 million and spawned Disney competitor DreamWorks Animation SKG when Katzenberg went into business with new partners Steven Spielberg and David Geffen. "If Frank Wells were alive, this never would have happened," the plaintiff's attorney said when the suit was filed.

When he finally hired Michael Ovitz as president and his "partner" in 1995, Eisner failed to fully advise the board of directors about Ovitz's hiring or compensation. From the beginning, Eisner undercut Ovitz's authority, removing divisions from his control. It cost Disney more than $120 million in severance when Eisner terminated Ovitz.

By the summer of 2001, Disney's finances had badly deteriorated, with its returns on assets, equity, and invested capital all down by more than 50 percent. Profits, which peaked in 1997 at $1.97 billion, fell to just $120 million in 2001. Disney stock, which traded above $40 per share less than a year before, fell to below $24 the day before the September 11 terrorist attacks shut down the market.

Eventually, Eisner lost the backing of his original sponsors. Stanley Gold and Roy Disney, who recruited Wells and Eisner as a team to boost the value of the company, finally determined Eisner by himself was at the center of the stock's decline. "No one ignores Michael's successes from 1984 to 1994," they wrote in a letter to the board of directors during the 2004 fight for control of the company. "The problem is, following the death of Frank Wells in 1994, the company's performance has been substandard. How long can Michael Eisner live on the company's accomplishments from 1984 to 1994?"

The question was answered in March 2004, when an unprecedented 43 percent of shareholders withheld their votes to re-elect Eisner to the board. Within a year-and-a-half, he was unemployed. After Eisner, Disney's board chose to separate the positions of CEO and chairman, making sure the company is led by two people, not one.

Once again, acetylene proved to be nowhere near as powerful without the oxygen.

Chapter Two

A Common Mission

*"A friendship founded on business is better
than a business founded on friendship."*

— John D. Rockefeller

IN THE LATE 1990S, A GROUP OF RESEARCHERS from
two universities and the U.S. Naval Warfare Center recruited
112 young men and women and paired them randomly to
see how well each partnership could fly a combat mission
in an F-16 flight simulator. All the "pilots" were given a
45-minute hands-on training session. For each pair,
one of the volunteers flew the plane. The other gathered
information, set airspeed, and called up different weapons
systems. Both could fire the weapons.

The pairs received conflicting objectives that forced them
to make difficult choices. They were told to survive enemy
fire, fly a predetermined route that covered four destination
markers called "waypoints," and shoot down enemy aircraft.
"This scoring scheme presented a strategic dilemma for
teams, as the three objectives were incompatible," wrote

the researchers. "For example, flying directly toward all waypoints placed the team in great risk and left little time for fighting enemy planes. Alternatively, actively engaging enemy planes left little time for reaching waypoints." There was no way to get to all the waypoints without encountering enemy aircraft because that was where the enemy planes were typically circling.

Going into the test, the pairs displayed differing levels of what the researchers called a "shared mental model" of the challenge. The scientists were curious to know not just how well each pair coordinated in completing the mission, but how well they cooperated, how well they assumed their separate roles, how much they liked the activity, and the intensity of their "team spirit."

Each pair flew six missions that took about 10 minutes. While the duos' performance improved with practice, those who were more "in sync" at the beginning continued to stay better focused through the missions. Partners who shared a similar view of the challenge did better than the other pairs throughout the experiment. Working together well, the scientists concluded, requires a common view of the mission "above and beyond simple shared task knowledge."

What is true for flying a simulated combat assignment applies to all of your collaborative endeavors. A common mission is the foundation for all partnerships.

Collaboration is more than friendship or collegiality, more than being in the same office or working for the same firm, more than proximity or mutual appreciation.

It occurs only when you and an ally strive for a definitive accomplishment — passing work between yourselves, "putting your heads together," or doubling up on a task neither of you could accomplish alone. For this reason, the relationship is unique. It exists to serve the goal. It lasts only until the mission is accomplished. Once the objective is reached, the partnership must adopt a new goal or it dissolves.

Although a strong friendship often emerges from collaboration, the partnership itself ends once there is no longer a shared, uncompleted objective facing the two people. Coauthors are partners until their book is finished. Astronauts are confederates only until the space mission returns to Earth. It's the active, unresolved case that makes partners of two fellow prosecutors.

Three statements from the Gallup research proved to be best at assessing the degree to which both people in a partnership are pursuing the same objective:

- We share a common goal.
- We have a common purpose for what we do.
- We believe in the same mission in life.

The thresholds are just as high on the common mission element as they are for the statements that apply to complementary strengths. Here too, respondents were asked to rate their agreement with each of these statements from 1 ("strongly disagree") to 5 ("strongly agree"). To be categorized as reaching a "good" level on having a common mission, respondents must average at least 3.6 on the three statements above. To be "exceptional," they must strongly agree to each one.

"As a teacher, I collaborate whenever possible," one woman said. "A colleague and I infused music into the U.S. history curriculum by spending a summer going to obscure libraries and listening to songs that reflected various events. We then created activities that went with each song. This partnership was so successful because we shared a common vision and we were working together on it from start to finish."

Although a shared mission is essential, maybe even obvious, the lack of this basic concurrence is where many pairs fail. Only one in four people in poor partnerships agree they have a common goal or purpose with the other person. In many cases, both think they are on the same page, but when limits of time, money, or attention force difficult choices, it becomes clear the two have conflicting priorities. Only 9 percent of those in poor partnerships say they were "very successful" at reaching their goal. It's difficult to do if you're not aiming at the same target.

Your primary qualification to participate in a partnership is your ability to help fulfill the mission the two of you share. The same is true of your counterpart. Therefore, the person you select as a collaborator is likely to be different than someone you would choose as a friend, date, neighbor, or roommate. However much you may like someone, think highly of his abilities, or admire her determination, you would be foolish to embark on a partnership unless both of you agree on the objective and bring something unique to its achievement.

Partnerships produce something more than just the happiness of the two participants. Two college roommates are not collaborators; two classmates working together on a paper for a shared grade are. Next-door neighbors are not partners, but they are if they team up to argue against their city's plan to extend the road on which they live. Two mothers of elementary-school-aged girls may be on cordial terms, but they are not a team until they volunteer to lead their daughters' Girl Scout troop.

Without a shared mission, partnerships inevitably break into two individual pursuits. With a common goal, two people who might otherwise knock heads subordinate their personal concerns for the sake of the accomplishment.

At 27,900 feet above sea level, Tenzing Norgay and Edmund Hillary were left alone to attempt the summit of Everest.

There were others with them earlier in the climb, carrying gear and oxygen bottles and cutting steps in the ice and snow. It took three months for the British expedition and their hired Sherpas to get the two men to Camp Nine. Then, on the afternoon of May 28, 1953, the support team descended, leaving Tenzing and Hillary just enough oxygen, food, and equipment to give them a chance at reaching the top.

"Tenzing and I watched them go, and I felt an intense feeling of loneliness as they slowly clambered down the mountain-side, leaving us on our little ledge," wrote Hillary. Whether the two men succeeded, and whether they survived, depended on how well they worked together on their common goal.

The partnership was not perfect. Tenzing would have preferred to climb with Swiss mountaineer Raymond Lambert, with whom he nearly reached the summit exactly a year before and whose red scarf he wore on this climb. But Nepal issued its single climbing permit in 1953 to the British, not the Swiss. (Even though Hillary was from New Zealand, he had been on previous British climbs and was invited to join the 1953 climb.) Hillary would have chosen George Lowe, one of the three men who had just descended, but expedition leader John Hunt would not allow it. "We had the rather sneaking feeling that John didn't really want two New Zealanders to stand on the top of Mt. Everest," said Hillary. Forced to find a new counterpart, Hillary teamed up with the respected Sherpa.

Yet these disappointments paled in comparison to Tenzing's and Hillary's dedication to reaching the highest point on Earth. To stand on the summit, both were willing to suffer the trials of high altitude, to risk their lives, and to relegate their selfish concerns. "I have always hated small bickerings and resentments while one is engaged on a great adventure," wrote Tenzing. "When people are going to a mountain they should forget the molehills. When they are involved in a big thing they should have big hearts to go with it."

Although there are, of course, endeavors that can be accomplished alone, in 1953, conquering Mt. Everest wasn't one of them. Two men were better than one. One man worked on the oxygen equipment while the other fired up the stove for meals and the hot, sugary lemonade that provided energy and fought off dehydration. Two people needed to set up the tent in the blasts of Himalayan wind. When working their way up the mountain, the men took turns leading, allowing the trailing climber an easier go of it.

The most important advantage two climbers have over one is the ability to rope themselves together and spread out. In precarious spots, only one ventures forward. The other secures himself and the rope in case the leading man falls. The technique is called a belay.

Belaying had already saved Hillary's life earlier in the expedition. He was in the lead as they navigated between towers of ice in the treacherous Khumbu Icefall. Without warning, the snow under Hillary's feet gave way, and he slid into a crevasse. "Tenzing! Tenzing!" he shouted. Tenzing jammed his ax into the snow and threw himself next to it as the rope unraveled and jerked taut between them. "Fortunately there was not too much rope between us, and I was prepared," said the Sherpa. "I was able to stop his fall after about 15 feet and then, with slow pulling and hauling, managed to pull him up again. By the time he was out of the crevasse my gloves were torn from the strain; but my hands were all right, and except for a few bruises Hillary was unhurt."

Mountaineers consider themselves one entity moving toward the summit — one "rope" — when tied together and climbing. Discussing similar falls when he was tied to Lowe, Hillary told an interviewer: "You could say he was saving my life every time, but we don't think of it in those terms. We were a team; someone had to go down first. And someone had to be second to make sure they didn't go to the bottom."

In 1953, no one knew for sure whether humans could reach the summit without succumbing to deadly high-altitude illnesses. Above 26,000 feet, there is so little oxygen in the air that a person can live only for a few days. George Mallory and his companion, Andrew Irvine, died near the top in 1924. Numerous attempts in the 1930s and 1940s ended in failure.

Hillary and Tenzing spent a difficult night at Camp Nine in hopes that sleeping at the higher altitude would put them within reach of the summit on the next day. "Everything took five times as long as it would have in a place where there was enough air to breathe," wrote Tenzing. They alternated between using bottled oxygen to allow them to sleep and waking to drink more lemonade. They awakened for good before 4 a.m. on the morning of May 29. The temperature was -25 degrees Celsius.

Emerging three hours later, Tenzing took the lead while Hillary's feet warmed inside his boots, which had frozen overnight. "Always willing to do his share, and more than his share if necessary, Tenzing scrambled past me and tackled the slope," recalled the New Zealander. When Hillary's feet began to warm, they reversed places, sharing the work of kicking steps into the snow.

The pair soon faced a choice: They could either proceed along a ridge or take a snow slope to its left. Hillary decided the slope was safer. "We were climbing up an almost vertical white wall," wrote Tenzing. "The worst part of it was that the snow was not firm, but kept sliding down, sliding down — and we with it — until I thought, 'Next time it will keep sliding, and we will go all the way to the bottom of the mountain.'"

Through the most difficult slopes, the two men changed the lead more frequently, picking their way higher until they found snow that provided safe belays. At one point, they found themselves facing snow cornices on the right hanging over a 10,000-foot drop and a precipice on the left overhanging an 8,000-foot fall. "It looks a fair cow, all right, as we'd say in New Zealand," Hillary recalled.

"If we were to get to the top," wrote his partner, "it would have to be along a narrow, twisting line between precipice and cornices: never too far to the left, never too far to the right — or it would be the end of us."

Having navigated the ridgeline, they took turns, each belaying the other as he wedged himself into "a kind of chimney" created by snow on one side and rock on the other. The exertion left each man "panting like a gaffed fish."

The angle was no longer as steep. The terrain appeared safe enough that the two men could walk together rather than taking turns. Uncertain about whether the snow would break off from the right, the climbers worked through a slope of snow on the left over a series of seemingly endless snow humps, each concealing the next.

"Suddenly I realize that the ridge ahead doesn't slope up, but down. I look quickly to my right," recalled Hillary. "There, just above me, is a softly rounded, snow-covered little bump about as big as a haystack. The summit." He turned to see his companion grinning through his oxygen mask. "I held out my hand, and in silence we shook in good Anglo-Saxon fashion. But this was not enough for Tenzing."

"This was not enough for Everest," recalled Tenzing. "I waved my arms in the air and then threw them around Hillary, and we thumped each other on the back until, even with the oxygen, we were almost breathless."

In the media frenzy that followed the men's accomplishment, reporters badgered the pair to know which of them reached the summit first. "All over the world I am asked, 'Who got there first? Who got there first?' Mountaineers understand that there is no sense to such a question," wrote Tenzing, "that when two men are on the same rope they are *together*, and that is all there is to it."

"All the way up and all the way down we helped, and were helped by, each other — and that was the way it should be," he explained. "We were not leader and led. We were partners."

ALTHOUGH YOU AND YOUR COLLABORATOR must agree on your mission, you don't need to have the same reasons for pursuing it. Successful partners often have different motivations for making the climb. This usually does not hinder the alliance, particularly if both of you understand the driving force motivating the other and work to see those hopes fulfilled.

In the last years of his life, Ulysses S. Grant needed money. He was bankrupt and suffering from terminal throat cancer. Mark Twain needed a bestseller for his fledgling publishing company. Their personal missions overlapped in their desire to see Grant's autobiography published. The two-volume *Personal Memoirs of U.S. Grant* was both a financial and literary success, a bestseller of its time that earned Grant's family more than $400,000 and strengthened Twain's company. Grant and Twain had disparate reasons for wanting to see the book published, but they agreed on what they planned to send to the printing presses.

Motivations are often unique and deeply personal things, which complicates the issue of agreeing on the goal. You can't assume your partner's motivations are the same as your own; there's a good chance they're not. One of you may see success on a major project as a chance to justify higher pay, while the other wants company-wide recognition. One attorney may want to win a big case to secure a promotion, while the other wants the chance to work on even larger cases. While one police officer likes locking up criminals, his partner most enjoys the daily interaction with law-abiding residents. In the best partnerships, both people not only agree on the mission, they understand why their counterpart finds it meaningful.

You must also be careful not to assume that because you and someone else have collaborated well in the past, you will do so in the future. Collaborating with the same person can be a dramatically different experience depending on the degree to which both of you are working for the same end. You must lay the foundation separately for each mission.

John Adams and Thomas Jefferson fell into this trap. As delegates to the Continental Congress, the two men were assigned to draft the Declaration of Independence for the young United States. Because they shared the same goal, they worked out their differences. They quibbled, most notably about which of them should do the writing, but they did so constructively. Jefferson wrote the document; Adams defended it before the Congress. Each made small sacrifices for the sake of the goal. Their common mission united them.

In 1796, America's first contested presidential election brought the men together again, but without a mutual objective and with predictable results. Adams was the candidate of the Federalists; Jefferson was the choice of the Democratic-Republicans. At that time, before the ratification of the 12th Amendment, the second-place candidate became vice president, regardless of his party. By an electoral vote margin of 71 to 68, Adams became president and Jefferson his vice president. They had a historic opportunity to collaborate again and to overcome party politics.

But this time, they had divergent views about how the new country should be run. Although Adams briefly put forward the idea of integrating Jefferson into his administration, nothing came of it. Although Jefferson wrote a heartfelt letter that may have bridged their partisan divide, he never sent it. Without a shared goal, neither made enough of the concessions that united them in their earlier work.

Jefferson recalled the day when it was clear their working relationship ended. On a Monday evening in March 1797, the two men had dinner with George Washington and happened to leave at the same time. Walking together, they had a brief discussion about whether to send James Madison — a member of Jefferson's party — to France, a friendly gesture by Adams that came to nothing because the Federalists disapproved and Madison declined. Adams withdrew the offer. "We came to Fifth Street," wrote Jefferson, "where our road separated, his being down Market Street, mine off along Fifth, and we took leave; and he never after that said one word to me on the subject, or ever consulted me as to any measures of the government." The president and his vice president went their separate ways that night and didn't collaborate for the next 15 years. This parting of the ways is inevitable when two people have divergent objectives.

The need for parallel aims is no less true for small projects than for those that make history. "My partner and I planned to complete a nature trail in the woods," said one man Gallup interviewed. "We thought we understood what needed to be done," he said, but they ultimately became discouraged and stopped working on the trail "because we did not see the big picture and the end goal clearly enough."

Another respondent complained her counterpart lacked the same intensity she had for a new electronic reporting system designed to save their company millions of dollars. "My partner could not visualize the importance of our task or was focused on other objectives," she said. Consequently, the project failed. "The difference in this partnership compared with successful ones I've had would be that I saw this as a cost saver for a billion-dollar operation, and she saw it as an unnecessary task."

How can two people be successful working together if they don't move toward the same objective? How can a canoe be paddled in two directions at once? While a shared goal alone is not enough to create a functional pair, without it, the two people are working at cross-purposes. A common mission unites disparate but complementary personalities. It elevates a working relationship above an arms-length negotiation, peaceful coexistence, or outright antagonism.

"I serve on the board of directors of my subdivision with a guy who is about 15 years older than me," said one man.

"We have very different management styles, and we often clash very hard when working on the board. However, last summer we were in agreement on whether our subdivision should be part of the city. We worked long and hard, gathering petitions from our neighbors about the 'cityhood' issue. We agreed on the objective, and by and large, we agreed on the process to achieve it. On this project, it was easy to get along with him. While at times we really hate each other personally, somehow we can put it aside and start anew when another project begins."

This level of agreement can make two people who would normally be adversaries into allies. Its absence can just as reliably generate friction and create failure between two people who otherwise seem to be natural friends.

Sojourner Truth and Olive Gilbert hated slavery and wanted to hasten its demise. That wasn't enough.

When the two women decided to work together on a book, they had substantially different ideas about the final volume. Because they lacked a shared focus, Truth and Gilbert created a collection of compromises, exchanges, and minor disagreements rather than the far more powerful book that could have been. Their story illustrates how even with the noblest intentions, lack of a common mission undercuts collaboration.

Sojourner Truth was a former slave once known as Isabella. In the mid-1840s, she had been free for almost two decades and was living in the Northampton Association of Education and Industry, a socialist community in Northampton, Massachusetts. Members of the association operated a silk mill and believed in equality between men and women and blacks and whites.

Olive Gilbert was a white abolitionist who was just a few years younger than Truth. Both women knew antislavery newspaper editor William Lloyd Garrison. He may have been the person Gilbert described as "a friend who had resided for a time in the 'Community,' and who, after describing [Truth], and singing one of her hymns, wished that [I] might see her."

Sometime after the failure of the Northampton Association, Truth bought a house and needed money to pay the mortgage. An itinerant preacher by this time, she also wanted to tell her life's story, but she was illiterate. Gilbert could read and write, and she wanted to use Truth's experiences to portray the horrors of slavery. At some point, they sat down to work on a book — the former slave telling her story, and the writer taking notes.

Isabella was born about 1797 in Ulster County, New York. Her first master was a Dutch immigrant, and Dutch became the girl's first language. Because of the selling of slave children from their parents and husbands from their wives, many of the most basic facts about Isabella's family were unknown to her. She believed she was the second youngest of 10 or 12 children, but her older siblings were sold before she could remember. She recounted a heart-wrenching story about her 3-year-old sister and 5-year-old brother being torn from their family.

Truth told the writer how she was sold at the age of 9 for $100 to a second master, and she remembered being auctioned along with a number of sheep. She spoke only Dutch, and her new owners spoke only English, so they struggled to communicate. When she failed to understand orders, her masters became angry, and at one point, they whipped her until she was deeply cut and badly bleeding. "And now," Truth told Gilbert, "when I hear 'em tell of whipping women on the bare flesh, it makes *my* flesh crawl, and my very hair rise on my head! Oh! My God! What a way is this of treating human beings?"

Gilbert portrayed Truth as a strong and eloquent woman. Although it was customary at the time to render quotes from uneducated blacks in broken vernacular, Gilbert quoted her collaborator in standard English. "This decision makes a tremendous difference in the dignity of the portrait she drew," wrote University of Massachusetts Professor Jean M. Humez.

In their conversations, Truth told Gilbert many terrible stories — how she lived in a dingy basement with a number of other slaves and how she was attracted to a slave named Robert from a neighboring property, but his master forbade him from visiting, "anxious that no one's property but his own should be enhanced by the increase of his slaves." She told the writer how her master broke his promise to free her a year before New York law required it, how she therefore claimed her own freedom by leaving, and how she had to sue to regain her illegally sold son.

A religious tone permeated Truth's stories, such as how she took the name Sojourner and felt prompted by God to travel on a religious mission east of New York. "What are you going east for?" asked one woman at whose house she was staying. She replied, "The Spirit calls me there, and I must go."

Narrative of Sojourner Truth: A Northern Slave was first published by Garrison in 1850. It allowed Gilbert, who would otherwise be unknown today, to editorialize against slavery in a way she never could have alone. The publication of the book made Truth a prominent abolitionist and speaker. Her fame eventually gained her a meeting with President Abraham Lincoln. She confessed she had not heard of him until he was running for the presidency. Lincoln smiled and replied, "I had heard of you many times before that."

Yet for all that *Narrative of Sojourner Truth* accomplished, the book is much less than what it could have been. It leaves the reader confused as to whether it is meant to be a story of one unique woman or an indictment of slavery. The text jumps from Gilbert narrating, to Truth speaking, to Gilbert dismissing her coauthor's perspective. *Narrative* is full of "internal strains," concluded historian Nell Irvin Painter. Through most of it, "Gilbert the abolitionist is often at odds with Truth the autobiographer."

Their book is "marred by [Gilbert's] tendency to interpolate her opinions into the text," wrote history professor Jeffrey C. Stewart. "Rather than let her subject speak without moralizing interjections, Gilbert seizes upon Sojourner's life story as a vehicle for her own indictment of slave owners and their justifications for slavery."

The women had "contrasting and often clashing agendas," wrote Humez. The finished work "implies a process of strenuous contest and negotiation between the two women" that led to "contradiction and even incoherence" in some of the most important passages of the book. It is impossible to fault either woman for her goal. Yet while both were worthy objectives, they were not sufficiently aligned to make a single, cohesive volume.

Without intending to do so, Gilbert and Truth taught lessons beyond the horrors of slavery and the compelling nature of a spiritual journey. They also showed that no matter how talented you and your collaborator may be, how complementary the fit between you, or how laudable your individual intentions, if you cannot agree on a common mission, your partnership will ultimately fall short of its potential.

Chapter Three

Fairness

"There is no such thing as justice in the abstract;
it is merely a compact between men."

— Epicurius

SEVERAL YEARS AGO, a scientist at Emory University introduced female capuchin monkeys to money. She gave them granite pebbles and taught them that if they surrendered a rock back to her, she would trade it for a piece of cucumber. Capuchins like cucumbers, and if that were the only deal available, they would trade rocks for cucumber slices almost every time.

The researcher then placed two monkeys in cages next to each other so they could see the bargain made by the capuchin next door. The primatologist approached one monkey and made the standard trade: a pebble for a piece of cucumber. Next, the scientist approached the second monkey and exchanged the pebble not for a cucumber slice, but for a grape. Capuchins like grapes more than they like cucumber slices.

Seeing another monkey get a better reward for the same action, the first capuchin often got upset. She might "go on strike," refusing to make the exchange in future rounds. She might refuse to eat the cucumber piece even though she paid a pebble to acquire it, and if she hadn't seen the grape trade, she would certainly have eaten it. In extreme cases, she might throw a small fit "such as tossing the token or reward out of the test chamber."

Behaving this way is irrational. The aggrieved monkey didn't hurt anyone but herself by refusing to trade rocks for food or by throwing away cucumbers she otherwise would have eaten. So why did she do it?

"Capuchin monkeys," wrote the authors of the study, "seem to measure reward in relative terms, comparing their own rewards with those available, and their own efforts with those of others. They respond negatively . . . if a partner gets a better deal." Academics call this phenomenon "inequality aversion" or "distributive justice." You might call it evenhandedness, doing right by the other person, or just plain fairness. If fairness is essential for a capuchin monkey, it must be more important and more basic to humans than we realize.

Gallup's research did not involve cucumbers, grapes, or side-by-side enclosures, but similar discoveries emerged nonetheless in interviews with people comparing their best and worst partnerships. Several statements about fairness proved crucial for successful collaboration. We asked respondents how strongly they agreed or disagreed with each of these statements:

- We share the workload fairly between us.

- We do not have to keep track of who does what and who gets credit for what.

- We see each other as equals — one is not better than the other.

Your partnership has little chance of succeeding unless both of you believe it is fair. On a scale from 1 ("strongly disagree") to 5 ("strongly agree"), it takes an average above 3.6 on these statements to reach the range considered "good." Only respondents who strongly agree to all three statements have excellent alliances.

Particularly at the beginning of a working relationship, colleagues cannot avoid making comparisons between their own rewards and those of their counterpart as they decide how earnestly to maintain the collaboration. Even if you have no formal authority over the pay, promotion, or recognition of your collaborator, you should make sure he gets a fair deal. If you are getting grapes, you have a responsibility to make sure your counterpart is getting something better than cucumbers.

On one level, fairness is just common sense. Imagine what would happen if a mother asked her two young children to work together to pick up their toys and then rewarded one child with an apple and the other with an ice cream cone. Moms understand fairness, and they know that "active rejection" from toddlers wouldn't be any more civilized than it would be from monkeys. "Any parent with two or more children needs no formal analysis to be persuaded of the importance of distributive justice," observed one pair of scientists.

As logical as the need for fairness may be, feelings of being used are often at the heart of what destroys a working relationship. This is especially true when one of the two people has the ability to impose terms on the other. When Gallup asked people whether they and their manager share the workload fairly between them, the answers tilted dramatically toward the negative end of the scale. Nearly one-third strongly disagreed. Only 16 percent strongly agreed.

Without any knowledge of terms like "distributive justice" and "inequality aversion," children quickly learn a series of conventions to maintain fairness. How should they split a piece of chocolate cake? One girl should cut it; the other gets to choose her half. Who gets to go first in a board game? Highest roll of the die starts. How do they choose teams for football? Two captains alternate drafting players. Who gets to ride in the front seat first? "Rock, paper, scissors — shoot!" Kids know the game will fall apart without these mechanisms. The offended player will announce, "That's not fair!" take his marbles, and storm home.

Worries about fairness arise immediately at the prospect of teaming up with someone else. One high school freshman was stunned when her father told her to expect a teacher to one day team her up with someone else on a term paper. "Do they really do that? What if you have to do all the work?" she asked. "What happens if they pair you up with someone who's a really bad writer and won't do anything?"

There is no evidence that adults outgrow a desire for equity and fair play when they leave the classroom for the cubicle. Although they may paper over their reactions because of office politics, posturing, or waiting for the opportunity to even the score, everyone harbors an inner monkey. Adults may be less likely to whine, throw vegetables, or have a public meltdown, but their responses when asked about getting too much of the work or too little of the reward betray the same kinds of feelings.

"Our project required the viewing of hundreds of slides and creating lectures that would go with the slides," one respondent told Gallup. "I found myself doing about 80 percent of the work. Since my evaluation was dependent on it, I felt I had to get it done even if I had to do most of the work myself. What it all comes down to is a sense of equity. If two people either work together or divide the work evenly, everything will be fine." She was so frustrated by the experience that she could not write they had "worked together" without putting the phrase in quotes.

When both people in a partnership work equally hard and split the rewards, comments from teammates sound much different: "My lab partner in my last biology class and I worked very well together. We were both good in the subject and good students, so there wasn't one person doing all the work. Neither of us had anything to prove or any ego wrapped up in the assignments, so we didn't care who did what. We were just laid-back. We both got A's in the class."

The wisest partners understand that all the maturity and diplomacy they display hides a core of more primitive reactions. In stressful circumstances, even when decisions are made fairly, comrades' emotions can threaten to derail the relationship.

In 1908, legendary explorer Ernest Shackleton and three other men on an Antarctic expedition — all four of them nearly starving — came upon a site where other expedition members had dropped three small pieces of chocolate and a piece of dog biscuit. Their established method for distributing food was for one man to turn his back while another pointed to a portion and asked, "Whose?" Because the man with his back turned could not see which portion he was assigning, the decisions were random — they were fair. This time, Shackleton got the piece of dog biscuit.

Although he was credited by all his men with incredible toughness and restraint, Shackleton confided in his journal his base motives just below the surface: "I was unlucky enough to get the bit of biscuit, and a curious unreasoning anger took possession of me for a moment at my bad luck. It shows how primitive we have become."

eBay founder Pierre Omidyar made an important equitable gesture when he brought Jeff Skoll on board as his partner in 1996. The men needed to decide how to divide ownership in the new business. Skoll, a Stanford MBA, made involved calculations of the value of the company and the contributions of the two partners. "He had all sorts of analyses," said the founder. Rather than strain at the details, they decided to use a simpler approach suggested by Omidyar. He estimated the work he performed before Skoll arrived to be worth 15 percent of the company's value. They split the rest evenly.

The sense of internal justice, although difficult to delineate in complex real-life interactions, is nonetheless fundamental for effectively working together. It can be taken for granted when present, but its absence will destroy your shared work. We are all simply grown-up, more civilized versions of the children we were decades ago, negotiating the rules of a sandlot baseball game or trading mowing the lawn one day for doing the paper route the next.

We adults usually aren't as explicit, but research indicates we also disengage and retreat if we feel as if someone is taking advantage of us. Much as the monkeys will throw an apparently self-destructive fit to protest unfairness, people also do irrational things when others violate their sense of justice. In a partnership, it's not what's smart or what's logical that matters, but what's equitable. The emotional reactions of collaborators drive them toward interacting fairly or not interacting at all.

✯✯

In August of 1937, two 24-year-old men sat down and wrote some notes about a business idea they had been discussing since their days together in college. At the top of the page, they wrote "Tentative organization plans and a tentative work program for a proposed business venture." The men kicked around ideas for electronic devices the business could manufacture. Perhaps they should make some high-frequency receivers. "We should make every attempt to keep up on television," they wrote to themselves. They planned to name their venture The Engineering Service Company.

It wasn't until two years later that the partners actually founded the enterprise. One of the men arranged for his recently married counterpart to rent the lower level of a house in Palo Alto, California, from an elderly woman who lived upstairs. The single guy moved into the small storage shed in the back. They made the house's one-car garage into their production facility and began taking on what was at first an odd assortment of projects.

They designed and built a controller to adjust the tracking speed of the telescope at a nearby observatory. They invented a device to show when a bowler crossed the foul line at a neighborhood bowling alley. A local entrepreneur hired them to create a tone generator to tune harmonicas and an "exerciser" to artificially stimulate muscles. The entrepreneur "had an accommodating wife," wrote one of the collaborators, "and we spent one Sunday applying electrical currents of different frequencies to activate her leg muscles."

As dubious as some of the first endeavors were, they brought in money and built the men's confidence in themselves. "They also revealed something we hadn't planned but that was of great benefit to our partnership — namely, that our abilities tended to be complementary," wrote one of them. His partner "was better trained in circuit technology, and I was better trained and more experienced in manufacturing processes. This combination of abilities was particularly useful in designing and manufacturing electronic products."

As it occurred to them they might have a real business on their hands, they signed a partnership agreement. One of the men loaned the enterprise some money to buy components and tools. The other contributed tools. They decided the name of their company was too generic; they should name it after themselves. But given that they considered themselves equals, whose name should go first? They flipped a coin. When it landed, the name of the company became Hewlett-Packard.

The coin flip between Bill Hewlett and Dave Packard is considered just an interesting anecdote among the larger legends of the company. The men made no big deal of it. Yet the simple method of decision making, reminiscent of playground customs, emerges surprisingly often in situations when one partner must be chosen over the other and neither wants to be perceived as elbowing out his compatriot. The coin flip is simple. It is objective. It lets Fate decide.

In equitable partnerships, the coin toss often emerges at a crucial juncture. In 1903, Orville and Wilbur Wright flipped a coin to decide who would get to fly their new airplane. Wilbur won, but he stalled and crashed. Three days later, his brother took the historic first flight. Like Hewlett and Packard, William Hanna and Joe Barbera flipped a coin to name their animation company. If heads, it would be Barbera and Hanna. If tails, it would be Hanna-Barbera. It was tails.

To keep things simple, one pair of Tacoma, Washington, real estate agents even wrote the coin flip into their legal papers. "I have a clause in my partnership agreement that should my partner and I ever disagree and feel so strongly that we cannot agree, then we have agreed to settle the issue by the toss of a coin," said one of them. They have yet to invoke the rule, "although we joke about it sometimes."

On the surface, settling a dispute with a coin flip may seem inconsequential. But in psychological terms, invoking simple, indisputably fair rules is deeply symbolic of the fairness of an alliance.

In the early years of Hewlett-Packard, fairness was also created by the sheer volume of work to be done. There were too many products to be made and too few employees for anything other than both men working as hard as they could. "Basically, we divided it," said Hewlett. "Packard had taken business courses in school and I had not. So he was more on the business side and I was more on the engineering side, but I have to say that is oversimplified. We both did both."

The way they manufactured one of their earliest products, an audio oscillator, was quaint compared to the international corporation Hewlett-Packard would become. "We bought the cabinets but made the panels ourselves," wrote Packard. "We sawed them out of aluminum and drilled the holes. Then we'd spray-paint them at home and use the kitchen oven to bake on the paint." (Packard's wife, Lucile, reportedly said food baked in the oven never tasted quite right after the appliance was co-opted for electronics production.) The panels were engraved at a friend's facility. The dials were calibrated, and the calibration marks were engraved over pencil markings the two men made carefully on each instrument. "In the beginning, each of these oscillators was individually calibrated," recalled Packard.

In 1939, the first full year of business, Hewlett-Packard booked $5,369 in revenue, clearing $1,563 in profits. The business continued to prosper, outgrowing the garage in Palo Alto, hiring employees, and expanding its product line.

During World War II, Hewlett, already a member of the U.S. Army Reserve, was called back into active service. He was absent from the company for nearly five years. Packard decreased his own compensation to match that of Hewlett's military pay. "I did not think it was fair for my salary to be higher than Bill's army salary," Packard concluded. Not only was it a substantial sacrifice, it was perfectly symbolic.

The fairness that Hewlett and Packard displayed toward each other was equally evident in their management practices, an approach that came to be known almost reverentially as "the HP Way." When one of the employees fell ill with tuberculosis, the company helped pay for his care. Then the two founders arranged to offer catastrophic healthcare insurance for their employees, an unusual benefit at the time. While some other companies paid production bonuses to their engineers, Hewlett and Packard decided to pay them to all employees.

As a matter of trust between the company and its employees, they instituted flexible work hours. "To my mind," wrote Packard, "flextime is the essence of respect for and trust in people. It says that we both appreciate that our people have busy personal lives and that we trust them to devise, with their supervisor and work group, a schedule that is personally convenient yet fair to others." They opened up bins that were previously locked as a precaution against theft. "Open bins and storerooms were a symbol of trust, a trust that is central to the way HP does business," opined Packard.

Rather than lay off employees during difficult times, they reduced the hours and pay of employees across the board so all of them could keep their jobs until demand picked up again. The two founders lectured their managers in company memos and in person, saying that by asking people to work for them, they created a moral obligation to the employees. Packard and Hewlett bought recreational property in the company's name and made it available for employees to use for camping. As the business grew, they held company parties at which the founders served the food to ensure that they could greet everyone.

"Over and over again, Hewlett and Packard faced business decisions that were, in the end, character choices," wrote Michael S. Malone in his book about the partners. "Because they were men of character, Bill and Dave almost always made great business choices. It was their ultimate fallback position — 'What is the right thing to do?' — in the face of ambiguous data and conflicting pressures from investors, employees, and customers."

The HP Way is revered as being enlightened and ahead of its time. What is less appreciated is how this management philosophy was a natural extension of the partnership between Packard and Hewlett, a relationship that was, above all, fundamentally fair.

★★

WHILE PEOPLE FIND FAIRNESS INSTINCTIVE, they struggle to define it. Pressed for a definition, most people get no closer than U.S. Supreme Court Justice Potter Stewart when challenged to define obscenity: "I know it when I see it." The confusion stems from the fact that fairness is as much an emotional conclusion as a rational one. And there are different, opposing forms of fairness that apply, depending on the situation.

The most basic form is equality, a 50-50 division of the work and the rewards. Such a perfect split rarely occurs in practice. Any objective measurement of the work two people put into a project or the rewards they get from it would find at least a slight imbalance. Yet the symbolic value of an even division is often the assumed starting point and the ideal to which both partners aspire. It is the magnetic North Pole of most collaborations — intuitively appealing and difficult to argue, which is why it emerges in so many successful pairs. When Gallup asked people about the division of work and rewards in their best partnerships, nearly half said they and their collaborators evenly split both the work and the rewards.

A powerful partnership does not need to be equal to be fair. There are many times when one member of a dyad does more of the work, brings a rare talent, has far more experience, or otherwise "deserves" — the term is unavoidably subjective — a larger share of the reward. A child who is upset about getting less pay for household chores usually settles down when reminded that her sister did more of the work. Giving identical benefits to those whose workloads differ substantially is as unfair as giving vastly different rewards for the same work.

In successful partnerships in which there is an uneven division of responsibilities, a corresponding division of rewards also occurs. You and your counterpart do not need to divide the work evenly, but you must make the rewards proportionate to the workload. Productive working relationships can be built on a 70-30 division of the work if there is a corresponding 70-30 division of the rewards. In the strongest relationships, there is even a certain degree of latitude or wiggle room. For example, some partners are happy doing 60 percent of the work and receiving just half the rewards.

There is a limit to this balance, according to Gallup's research. If you are doing less than 20 percent of the work, you are the other person's helper or assistant, not his partner. Of course, there are times in every collaboration when one of the pair is doing most or all of the work. Shifting the burden back and forth is common and productive, just as Edmund Hillary and Tenzing Norgay took turns taking the lead up Everest. But all back and no forth will destroy the relationship.

Alliances that leave one person shouldering too much of the load for too little of the reward fall into a zone almost exclusively populated by failed collaborations. "My least successful partnership was randomly established. We were to complete assessments for children in grades three and five that were aligned with the state-wide test," said one teacher. "The partnership failed because the other person did not show up to discuss and plan for the project, nor did she complete her part of the assessments. I completed 80 percent of the work on my own and had to revise her portion significantly before going to press. The primary difference between this partnership and a successful one was her level of dedication. After my 'partner' in the endeavor failed to meet her end of the agreement, I lost all professional respect for her and could not trust that her work would represent the level of professionalism to which I am accustomed."

Creating an equitable collaboration is further complicated by the fact that we're not very good at estimating our relative contributions to a shared project. You probably believe you've done a larger share of the work than you really have. Your partner probably suffers from the same egocentric bias.

In 1979, two researchers from the University of Waterloo in Ontario, Canada, recruited 40 men from an introductory psychology class. The researchers told the men they were testing how well two people could brainstorm ideas to combat smoking. The men were asked to work together on defining the problem, generating ideas, discussing the alternatives, selecting a solution, and explaining their rationale. The subjects were told their work would be forwarded to the government's Committee for the Prevention of Cigarette Smoking. Half were instructed to keep notes of their own contributions to the discussion. The other half kept notes of their partners' ideas.

Two or three days later, each participant was brought back alone, asked to look over his notes, and then interviewed about "who tended to control the course and content of the discussion" in the first session. Regardless of whether participants made notes about themselves or the other students, they gave themselves the majority of the credit. The average test subject took 57 percent of the credit for generating ideas, 53 percent for evaluating those ideas, 57 percent for creating the final proposal, and 59 percent for the overall discussion. "Individuals tend to accept more responsibility for a joint product than other contributors attribute to them," wrote the Waterloo researchers. "This is a pervasive phenomenon."

To make your partnership fair, you will need to keep in mind that although you are aware of everything you do for the joint effort, much of what your partner does escapes your notice. If you are like most people, you also have an inflated opinion of the value of your contributions. Selfishness and the natural bias toward believing one has done more than a comrade creates a pothole in the road of many joint projects. "It is this proportionality — this fairness — that determines people's satisfaction with their social and business interactions," concluded one study. "But if people consistently overestimate their own contributions, they may feel they are doing more than their share — and that others are doing less than theirs."

The Gallup partnership surveys found a similar pattern, but with a positive twist. In pairs that worked well, the average participant estimated that he did 54 percent of the work (meaning, of course, that he believed his counterpart did the remaining 46 percent). However, the average participant also believed he got 55 percent of the rewards. The two numbers are elegantly proportionate. Although it is impossible for both people's actual work to add up to more than 100 percent (54 + 54 = 108) or for the separate rewards to have exceeded the whole (55 + 55 = 110), the perceptions of the two collaborators don't have to comply with the laws of mathematics. In this case, it's the near equality of the work and reward percentages for each partner (54 ≈ 55) that matters most.

The average participant in a poor partnership, however, estimated she did 71 percent of the work and got only 41 percent of the rewards. There's no telling whether those numbers are a true reflection of relative contribution and payoff. Those most likely to label a partnership as poor could, indeed, have gotten the raw end of the deal. It's also likely that when a working relationship is bad, the natural egocentric bias is magnified. More than either statistic by itself, it is the perceived mismatch of work and rewards (71 > 41) that poisons the relationship.

To be a great partner, you must continuously consider how much of the work your counterpart is shouldering and what she is getting for the effort. What rewards are most meaningful to her, and is she receiving them? Would you be willing to trade your work and rewards for hers? Are you truly working as equals? Addressing these issues requires candid conversations and a willingness, if needed, to take on more of the work for less of the rewards. Your collaborator needs to be similarly accommodating to you. Only when both partners are assured the other is more invested in the common mission than in a selfish pursuit do they, as the survey statement says, "not have to keep track of who does what and who gets credit for what."

Reaching this level is difficult even for society's most highly educated members. Professors often squabble over who gets what. Their spats are not over grapes and cucumbers, but over who gets her name first on a published paper. Professors with last names that start with letters at the end of the alphabet say it's not fair that they usually end up being listed second in journals that list authors in alphabetical order.

"Alphabetic name ordering ... which is the convention in the economics discipline and various other disciplines, is to the advantage of people whose last name initials are placed early in the alphabet," states a paper with a title right out of Dr. Seuss: "The Benefits of Being Economics Professor A (and not Z)." "As it turns out," the article continues, "Professor A, who has been a first author more often than Professor Z, will have published more articles and experienced a faster growth rate over the course of her career as a result of reputation and visibility. Moreover, authors know that name ordering matters and indeed take ordering seriously."

Capuchin monkeys know how to solve this problem. In 2006, researchers paired up the primates and put them in a device that held two food cups, one for each monkey. The cups remained out of reach unless both exerted their strength to draw them within reach. The researchers put their subjects in a dilemma by sometimes loading one cup with an apple slice and one cup with the more desirable reward of a grape. Just like being the first-named author on an academic paper, only one of the collaborators could have the grape during a particular round.

But the capuchins could switch sides. And that's just what the best partners did. The primatologists discovered that some of the teams — they labeled them "equitable pairs" — were better at taking turns being on the grape side of the mechanism, and by doing so, they were more successful. The other dyads, the "inequitable pairs" in which one monkey hogged the grape side, were more likely to fail when the monkey who rarely got the grape eventually refused to participate.

The capuchins changed how well they worked together "contingent on the equity of their interactions with their partner," wrote the scientists. "Dyads in which both individuals regularly alternated taking the higher value reward were more than twice as successful overall than less-equitable dyads." Monkeys smart enough to alternate who got the grape cooperated to get themselves two to three times as much fruit.

Such are the benefits of playing fair.

Chapter Four

Trust

"For when the One Great Scorer comes to mark
against your name, He writes — not that you won
or lost — but how you played the Game."

— U.S. sportswriter Grantland Rice

To TEACH POLICE CADETS how to search a dark building
without getting shot, the Arizona Law Enforcement
Academy puts people armed with paintball guns inside a
building. They hide behind furniture or in closets, waiting
for the trainees to flush them out. The instructors then send
in pairs of recruits suited up in pads that protect them from
direct hits.

The goal is to find and disarm each suspect before he
can "kill" or "wound" an officer. This doesn't always work out
as planned.

"During one of the drills, I was on one knee peeking into
a dark room while my partner pointed a flashlight into the
room from over my head," one cadet reported on his blog. "He
then pointed the light directly down on my head. He thought

he turned it off first. The suspect in the room immediately saw me and shot me in the hand. Even though we were in full pads, my fingers were unprotected. It is a painful place to get hit. I'm now sporting a colorful welt and blister on my index finger as a reminder of my partner's great tactics."

Five months later, the same cadet, now a Phoenix police officer, stopped a car with an invalid license plate. Two men were inside the vehicle. "One of my squad mates saw me pull over the car and pulled in behind me to provide backup," he wrote. "I approached the driver's window and asked him for his license. He said he had no identification. The passenger was hiding one of his hands under his leg. I told him to let me see his hands. My backup officer walked up to the passenger side, and we both knew there was something wrong."

The initial search turned up a gallon-sized freezer bag of marijuana in the back seat and a bag of cocaine in the passenger's pocket. With both suspects in handcuffs, the officer returned to the car to search it further. "I walked back to the passenger side of the car and felt my heart start racing when I saw a 9mm Ruger handgun sitting between the front seats partially under a piece of paper," he wrote. "The hammer of the gun was cocked back, and it was loaded. It would have taken two seconds for the passenger to pick it up if he had wanted to." A second loaded gun was hidden between the driver's seat and the center console.

"I had two guys committing serious felonies with loaded guns within reach," wrote the rookie. "If my backup partner hadn't arrived a few seconds after I did, I wonder if the outcome may have been different. Two [of them] against one [officer] may have encouraged them to take a chance with running or even shooting."

Every partner needs to be able to depend on his counterpart. Every partner takes a risk that the other person might fail, intentionally or innocently, leaving him with the light shining on him in the middle of a dark room. Every partner needs the dependable backup that is the difference between success and failure.

This came through forcefully in Gallup's analysis of people's responses about their best and worst partnerships. Three statements about trust form the heart of the working relationship:

- We trust each other.
- We can count on each other to do what the other says he or she will do.
- He or she tells others how good I am, and I tell others how good he or she is.

In a good collaboration, 58 percent of partners strongly agree that they trust each other, and another 29 percent score the statement a 4 on a 1-to-5 scale. In a poor partnership, less than 3 percent strongly agree they trust each other, while 50 percent strongly disagree.

Trust is the linchpin of a partnership. With trust, both people can concentrate on their separate responsibilities, confident the other person will come through. One brain-imaging study discovered that once trust is created, a person's brain will process his counterpart's cooperative move before it even happens.

Without trust, it's better to work alone. Both people doubt whether the other will fulfill his end of the bargain. Both must verify the other's actions. Both must make contingency plans in case their counterparts fail. The frustration and inefficiency of not being able to count on someone is more hassle than the burden of handling the full load alone. No trust, no partnership.

You face a dilemma every time you interact with someone new. If he can be trusted, and if he learns to trust you, the two of you can be more successful working together than going it alone. But if one of you is not trustworthy, it's better that you never even try to collaborate. This psychological fork in the road is one of the most important decisions a person makes. It's one of the crucial reasons humans can distinguish so many faces and keep track of so many reputations. For our ancestors living under more dangerous conditions, making the wrong choice could be fatal. For us, success on a project, reputations, promotions, future opportunities, happiness, and careers all hang in the balance.

Much of what we understand about trust is based on a simple experiment that has been replicated thousands of times, analyzed endlessly, made into a TV game show, and even factored into the United States' military decisions during the Cold War.

Imagine you are paired with a stranger to play the following game. You receive an empty red envelope. The other person receives an empty blue envelope. The instructor tells both of you to secretly place either $100 of your own money or nothing inside your envelope. Then he will take both envelopes, double whatever money he finds in each, and return them, but only after switching them so that you get the blue envelope and your counterpart gets the red one.

Would you put $100 in the red envelope? It's a simple question with a complicated answer — one of the most powerful inquiries in the research on human behavior. The question starkly illustrates the issue of trust. Your answer cuts to the essence of who you are as a collaborator.

There are four outcomes to this experiment:

Mutual trust: If you both risk your money, you both double your investment. You make $100, and so does your ally. This is the only way you both come out ahead.

Your counterpart betrays you: If you risk your money, but the other person puts in nothing, you'll lose $100, and he or she will gain $200. Your trust is abused, and you end up on the losing end.

You betray your counterpart: Should you fail to put in the money and the other person does, you gain $200 while risking nothing. This is the most profitable short-term strategy and therefore a real temptation, but you can employ it only by abusing the trust of your counterpart.

Mutual betrayal: If both of you risk no money, neither of you will lose any. But from your reticence or competitiveness, you both lose the chance to multiply your funds.

It's a serious predicament. If you are like most people, your mind is awash in questions. Who is this other person? Is there any indication you cannot trust him? Which would you prefer: the risk of being suckered or the chance you will burn your counterpart by wrongly assuming he wasn't going to play along? Even if you knew he was going to put $100 in the envelope, would you put in nothing? How would you play the game if there were many rounds with the same person? What assumptions do you make about those with whom you interact?

This is the partner's dilemma. No matter what the other person does, you are selfishly better off by investing nothing. But if you both follow cold calculations to this logical conclusion, there's no reason to even play.

Variations on this game have been played since the 1950s, when Princeton University mathematician Albert W. Tucker, looking for a way to illustrate a similar puzzle developed by two fellow researchers, created a story about two prisoners who were arrested together and interrogated separately by the police. The simple math behind the so-called "prisoner's dilemma" describes everything from two employees teamed up by their manager to the standoff between the United States and the Soviet Union in the last half of the 20th century. The scheme spawned thousands of articles about how humans determine when to trust each other in the face of many reasons to be untrusting or selfish.

In these dilemmas, as in real life, collaboration occurs only when both people trust each other and prove themselves trustworthy. This is a risky undertaking. Trust involves exposing yourself to the chance that the other person will fail to keep her end of the bargain.

The American TV game show *Friend or Foe?* created a partner's dilemma by squaring off two contestants whose trustworthiness determined how they would divide money they won together earlier in the show. Each had two buttons the other person could not see — one labeled "friend," the other "foe." If both players pushed "friend," they split their winnings evenly. If both pressed "foe," they both went home empty-handed. But if one pressed "friend" and one pressed "foe," the defector got all the money, and his partner received nothing.

One episode brought back two contestants who were betrayed in earlier shows, but who had accumulated $7,500 working together. "Mike, playing the game with you has been fun, and I think you are a trustworthy person," said fellow player Rob, putting his hand over his heart. "I'm giving you my word of honor that I will press 'friend.'"

"Rob, we've both been here before, and it would be a shame to go away with nothing," Mike reassured his counterpart.

They reached down and made their choices. Rob voted "friend." Despite his reassurances, Mike chose "foe," taking all the money for himself.

"I'm sorry," he said as the show's host berated him. "I couldn't be sure. I couldn't be sure."

"Things happen," said a clearly angry Rob. "Maybe you'll have a conscience sometime in the future. . . . All the money in the world can't buy you a clean conscience."

Betrayal — often mutual betrayal — was quite common on *Friend of Foe?* "Thousands of dollars were left on the table," wrote University of Chicago researcher John A. List. "In nearly 25 percent of the 117 games, both players chose not to cooperate, resulting in a net loss of nearly $100,000." Half the time, one of the players burned a cooperative partner, despite friendly overtures.

Occasionally, however, mutual trust made both people richer. "I think we worked really well together. I have a really good feeling about you," a contestant named Stacia told her counterpart, Jennifer. "We are both good people; I can just tell. It's better for both of us to go home with half the money than one or the other to be broke."

"Stacia, the other two teams voted 'foe' and walked away with nothing," replied Jennifer. "Let's go home feeling good about ourselves and with some money."

They both voted "friend" and split the money. "See," said the show's host, "nice people play *Friend or Foe?* too. They're not all evil little back-stabbers." The same lesson is true in real life.

In a working relationship, being trustworthy is not a matter of putting $100 in an envelope or hitting the right button. It is showing up for an important meeting on time, doing more than your share of the work, quickly returning e-mails and phone calls, giving all your creativity to a project, jumping in rather than having to be asked, not being a burden to your partner, fighting for the success of the project, working hard on physical jobs and smart on mental ones, and hundreds of other acts large and small.

In the early stages of a collaboration, both partners take a wait-and-see attitude, still in the clutches of the dilemma, not sure the other person is going to do his part. But if one cooperative move is matched by another, solid reputations form. The fear of being taken advantage of fades. Trust removes doubt. Trust eliminates the dilemma.

⋆⋆

NORWEGIAN LIV ARNESEN and American Ann Bancroft were both accomplished polar explorers in their own right when Bancroft wrote to Arnesen proposing that they team up to walk, ski, and sail across Antarctica. But they had never collaborated before. They had never even met.

Bancroft was the first woman to cross both the Arctic and Antarctic ice to reach the North and South poles. Arnesen led the first women's crossing of the Greenland Ice

Cap completed without supply depots along the way. She was the first woman to ski solo and without depots to the South Pole. "I skied to the South Pole alone simply because I couldn't find anyone to go with me," wrote Arnesen. "The men who were planning trips did not want a woman on their teams; and the female sport skiers I talked to were not interested in the extended camping and harsh weather of an Antarctic trip."

In the fall of 1998, Arnesen boarded a plane to Minnesota so she and Bancroft could each determine whether the other would make a suitable counterpart on an arduous three-month journey largely beyond the reach of help from anyone else. "I hadn't come with any expectations of what I thought she would be," recalled the Norwegian. "I did have some idea of what I hoped she would *not* be: a publicity hound, or a chatter-box, or perhaps someone who was more in love with the idea of expeditions than the trips themselves. I had encountered all these types during my various searches for expedition partners over the years. Good expedition members are hard to find."

Some people with whom Arnesen traveled before "who seemed strong and resilient cracked from the pressure of harsh weather and isolation, leaving the remaining team members to wake them and dress them and strap their skis on for them every day," wrote Arnesen.

Bancroft needed to know whether she had found someone on whom she could rely to save her life, whose degree of determination would mean the difference between success and failure. Assuming the woman standing in the baggage area of the Minneapolis airport with penguin stickers on her suitcase was Arnesen, Bancroft approached her. "I think I said something brilliant such as, 'Uh, hello. Are you Liv?' I was really thinking, 'Can I trust you?'"

The Norwegian also had doubts. "She looked skinny," recalled Arnesen, "and I remember thinking, 'Is she strong enough for an expedition like this?'" The visitor offered a handshake. "You must be Ann," she said.

Their concerns soon melted. The two former schoolteachers discovered they had a lot in common. Despite being raised an ocean apart, they had remarkably similar childhoods and dreams about the polar regions of the world, immersing themselves in books about explorers such as Roald Amundsen and Ernest Shackleton. "I just wanted to be there," said Bancroft. "I wanted to be in those pictures, in those grubby clothes and with those dogs on the ice. I wanted all of that adventure."

Arnesen's doubts about Bancroft's strength disappeared on a walk the next day when the Norwegian realized that, although small, the American was a powerful athlete. Her worries about Bancroft talking too much were also settled. As much as they enjoyed getting to know one another, "I noticed right away that we could also be comfortably silent," said Arnesen.

They talked about Shackleton and about their eagerness to face the same kind of tests he did. Bancroft talked about her dyslexia, her struggle to get a teaching certificate, and her hope of creating online lessons based on the expedition. The American said she looked at being an adventurer "as still being a teacher, but with a much bigger classroom."

"That was the moment I decided for certain to join the team," said Arnesen. Later that week, she repeated to the larger team what she told her husband in a phone call on her first day in Minnesota: "I had found more than my next expedition; I had found my *søstersjel*, my sister soul."

An expedition across Antarctica requires more of a partnership than does an alliance closer to civilization. Each woman had to rely on the other to pull a 250-pound sled loaded with food, a stove, fuel, skis, tents, assorted gear, sails, first aid kits, communication equipment, and navigation tools. As part of their preparation, they used a pig's foot to practice sewing up a deep laceration. "Stuff that's no big deal here could be catastrophic in the wilderness," said an emergency doctor who helped the two assemble their medical supplies. With little privacy and no one else around, every action had to be taken with consideration for how it would affect the other.

The trek lived up to its fearsome billing. The Antarctic broke sled poles, generated storms that made it impossible to see, battered their limbs, and sent them into bouts of depression when the weather halted their progress. Both women suffered frostbite and worried they might lose their fingers to the cold.

"So far, no difference of opinion. If we begin deviating, we discuss and decide," Bancroft wrote three weeks into the journey. "The cooperation between us goes very well," Arnesen wrote during the seventh week. Researchers who studied the partnership as it unfolded noted they had seen an expedition of two men under similar circumstances turn into traveling antagonism, the men motivated to continue by their hostility toward each other. But Arnesen and Bancroft were united by the educational goals of the mission and the hope it would provide a powerful example for schoolchildren.

The Antarctic unavoidably put a strain on the women's working relationship. At one point during the trek, Bancroft pulled hard on the line to her sail just as a large gust of wind hit the fabric. The force yanked her arm outward, tearing a muscle in her right shoulder. "The pain in the front of my right shoulder was excruciating and felt as if someone had jabbed a hot poker into my body," she recalled.

"I knew Ann was badly hurt," wrote Arnesen. "I didn't see her fall, but her body language was unmistakable. She was in desperate pain." The Norwegian wondered if her partner was refusing to acknowledge the severity of her injury. Over the next two days, the pair made good progress, sailing and skiing more than 66 miles, but Bancroft's injury forced them to stop roughly every half hour. Unbeknownst to Arnesen, the American was struggling with feelings of guilt about letting down her counterpart.

"Though I knew I had to talk to her about her injury, I wasn't sure how," recalled Arnesen. "So my way of showing her that I knew she was hurt was to offer help." During one of their breaks, Arnesen brought Bancroft something to drink and, seeing she was having some trouble getting unclipped from the sled, helped her get free of it.

"Listen!" Bancroft exploded, "I'm not one of the helpless tourists on your trips to Svalbard! I'm perfectly capable of managing on my own!" Angry and hurt, Arnesen set down the thermos she brought her teammate and walked back to her own sled, trying to keep her temper in check.

"Ann, I *know* you are capable, and I didn't mean to imply that you weren't," Arnesen said after the pain in Bancroft's arm forced them to stop for the day. "I'm just trying to be helpful because I know you are hurting." Bancroft apologized for her outburst, explaining that she felt patronized. They joked and laughed, cracking the wind-dried skin on their faces.

"I think we misunderstood each other sometimes so thoroughly that we were almost on two different expeditions," wrote Arnesen.

During their three months on the ice, the women agonized over the lack of wind they needed to cover the distance before the Antarctic summer ended. They fretted over gear that broke and the unforgiving terrain. Yet each was concerned about not letting down her partner. In circumstances that would put any relationship to one of its most severe tests, the women stuck together. Although "we each had our ways of getting on the other one's nerves," they trusted each other and proved themselves trustworthy.

While the partnership was strong, the wind was not. Arnesen and Bancroft did not cross all of Antarctica, but they did cover the entire land mass beneath the ice — more than 1,700 miles in 94 days — in temperatures that ranged from 14 to -31 degrees Fahrenheit. Their intense disappointment was tempered by the fact that an estimated 3 million children on five continents followed their progress and cheered them on.

After making the difficult decision to stop, the adventurers agreed to be patched in by telephone to a group of third-, fourth- and fifth-graders in Faribault, Minnesota. Already at their low point, the women were concerned they would be talking with a group of disappointed kids. Instead, the students talked about how the expedition had enlivened their studies. They took turns asking questions. They sang a song they wrote for the women.

Then a boy named Logan came to the phone and, putting aside the index card on which he had written a question, said, "I just wanted to tell you that both of you have been real role models to me. Sometimes I have a hard time with school, and I just used to feel like there were things I could never do. And now that you guys have done this, I see that I can do anything I put my mind to. You changed my life."

Before leaving the ice, Bancroft and Arnesen got the chance to visit Shackleton's hut at Cape Royds. "It was like coming full circle," wrote Bancroft. "We had a chance to walk into the very pictures we had pored over as girls dreaming of Antarctica."

"I felt as though I had been sent back in time and dropped into the pages of one of my well-worn childhood books," wrote Arnesen.

The question Ann and Liv asked themselves at the airport — "Can I trust you?" — was answered.

★★

MORE THAN 350 YEARS AGO, the philosopher Thomas Hobbes concluded that the incentives to be selfish when dealing with someone else are too strong to be resisted. He would have told you to put nothing in the envelope because the other person was almost certainly going to do the same.

The incentives in life naturally pull people toward "war of every man against every man," he wrote. As each person pursues his or her selfish interests, human existence is doomed to be "solitary, poor, nasty, brutish, and short."

Nobel Prize winner John Nash, portrayed in the movie *A Beautiful Mind*, looked for the patterns of behavior into which games of trust would settle if each player did what was best for himself. The "Nash Equilibrium," as it's called, of the envelope experiment is for both people to withhold their money every time.

John von Neumann, one of the pioneers of this type of strategic thinking, even recommended the United States launch a nuclear strike against the Soviet Union before the Soviets struck first. Agreeing with von Neumann, his contemporary Bertrand Russell argued a first strike was "as simple and as unescapable as a mathematical demonstration."

For many decades, educated theorists dismissed people who are trusting as just too stupid to really understand the game. "Evidently," concluded one book on the subject, "the run-of-the-mill players are not strategically sophisticated enough to have figured out that strategy DD [mutual defection] is the only rationally defensible strategy."

And, of course, every experienced collaborator has several stories of serious breaches, when trust was repaid with treachery, when perhaps Hobbes and Nash and von Neumann were right. At one retail firm, the highly effective partnership between two regional vice presidents, one responsible for the west half of the United States and the other responsible for the east, ended when one of them resigned and joined a competitor. "I invested a lot in him, and this is how he repays me?" said the one left behind. "To hell with him."

In the midst of this cynicism, political scientist and professor Robert Axelrod organized a curious competition. In 1979, Axelrod decided to use computers to seek the best strategy for when to extend and when to withhold one's trust. He invited experts to submit programs that were, in essence, a set of rules stating when a player would cooperate and when it would defect in a series of interactions similar to the envelope experiment.

Fourteen people agreed to participate in the tournament. They came from the disciplines of psychology, economics, political science, mathematics, and sociology. "Most of the entrants were recruited from those who had published articles on game theory in general or the prisoner's dilemma in particular," wrote the professor. No one could claim they were "not strategically sophisticated enough" to understand the power of being distrustful. They submitted a diverse group of strategies. Just like the variety of potential partners you encounter in any setting, the programs included jerks, saints, and many permutations in between.

The winner of the tournament turned out to be the simplest of all the programs. It was submitted by Russian-born psychologist Anatol Rapoport. Called "Tit for Tat," it began by cooperating on the first move, and then it just mimicked what its counterpart did on the previous move. In its simplicity, Tit for Tat was an elegant solution to the trust problem. It had several features of a good human partner that made it most successful in the tournament.

It got things off on the right foot by displaying trust on the beginning move, and unless it was betrayed, it never proved untrustworthy. In these ways, Tit for Tat and the others that performed best in the contest were not what Hobbes or Nash or von Neumann would have predicted. "Surprisingly, there is a single property which distinguishes the relatively high-scoring entries from the relatively low-scoring entries. This is the property of being *nice*, which is to say never being the first to defect," wrote Axelrod. When two trusting strategies met each other, they formed an elementary partnership, cooperating through almost the entire game, raising each other's scores along the way.

While it was friendly, Tit for Tat was no fool. As soon as it was betrayed, it retaliated on the next move and would continue refusing to cooperate until the other player ceased the hostilities. Because of this reflex, the strategy was "not very exploitable," wrote Axelrod. Such a fallback is crucial to the survival of otherwise obliging individuals. Without retaliation to keep them in check, just a few egotists or attackers can quickly overrun a benevolent population. Appealing to a sense of fair play works with most people, but a pernicious minority will exploit their colleagues' trust if nothing stands in their way.

Another winning feature of Tit for Tat was that as fast as it went to battle stations, it just as quickly returned to trusting when its counterpart did so. It was forgiving. "Of all the nice rules, the one that scored lowest was also the one that was least forgiving," Axelrod found.

The professor decided to try the experiment again, distributing the results of the first tournament to drum up additional interest. He wanted to know if more players and a wider variety of strategies could improve the results. Axelrod invited the initial set of players to try again. He also took out ads in computer journals. The response was more than he anticipated. Sixty-two entries came in from the United States, Canada, Great Britain, Norway, Switzerland, and New Zealand. They came from professors of computer science, physics, economics, psychology, mathematics, sociology, political science, and evolutionary biology. One came from a 10-year-old kid.

There were more than a million moves in the second tournament. All those who entered a strategy knew Tit for Tat won the first tournament, and why. Yet when all the strategies had a chance to interact with each other, the winner was once again Rapoport's simple rule, which he resubmitted unaltered from the first tournament. "So Tit for Tat, which got along with almost everyone, won the second round of the tournament just as it had won the first round," wrote Axelrod. It is "clearly a very successful strategy," he concluded.

The lesson in Axelrod's tournament lies in how forcefully it contradicts the supposedly savvy strategy of being selfish. Hobbes was wrong. Nash was wrong. Von Neumann, thankfully, was wrong. People are not purely selfish and calculating; they are reciprocating, both positively and negatively. They reflect what they receive. Reciprocity is one of the most powerful forces in human nature. In many ways, Axelrod's tournament confirmed the wisdom of a passage in the *Edda*, a 13th-century collection of Norse epic poems. "A man ought to be a friend to his friend and repay gift with gift," it states. "People should meet smiles with smiles and lies with treachery." The positive side of these deep-rooted emotions is the glue that holds together a partnership.

The most important element in forming and maintaining a variety of strong partnerships is not your craftiness, but your willingness to take the risk of trusting numerous potential partners and your diligence in repaying the trust they place in you. If you're not careful, you could be so "strategically sophisticated" that no one wants to work with you or that you fail to recognize or reciprocate collaborative overtures from people all around you. Just like Tit for Tat, you need to be eager to cooperate; to make early, friendly overtures to your partner; to stubbornly refuse to make the first hostile or neglectful move; and to be quite willing to forgive.

The ultimate twist to the research on trust is what it reveals about your collaborative environment. If you are like most people, you assume you are simply making reasonable reactions to the people with whom you interact. You believe you are working with the hand you were dealt. To the degree you compete, you probably feel as though you are just reacting to the competition around you. You probably attribute your lack of partnerships to a lack of good partners. But in a Tit for Tat world, where most people return good for good and bad for bad, the world you inhabit is the world you make.

Your reputation precedes you, biasing the way new colleagues deal with you. Your first moves, friendly or hostile, tip the balance for future interactions. When you exhibit trust, you will most often find trustworthiness. When you are selfish, you will most often find selfishness. When you compete, others must resort to competition. If you choose to play the game strictly for your own advantage, your attempts at collaboration will indeed be "solitary, poor, nasty, brutish, and short."

In the end, the degree to which you succeed in forming trusting partnerships is less a reflection of how much people trust you than how much you trust them — less a reflection of their trustworthiness than of your own.

Chapter Five

Acceptance

*"Admiration, n. Our polite recognition of
another's resemblance to ourselves."*

— Ambrose Bierce

ONE FACT ABOUT PARTNERSHIPS is so uncomfortable that your first reaction probably is to deny it: You form partnerships fastest and easiest with people most like yourself. Deep-seated biases make you more trusting of those who look most like you, who think like you, or with whom you have the most in common, whether you're from the same town, attended the same school, are fans of the same team, or mirror each other on more controversial factors such as race, age, religion, or sex.

As much as people like to think of themselves as equal-opportunity collaborators, the research demonstrates they are not, at least at first. Researchers in the 1920s and 1930s began documenting what even casual observers realize: schoolchildren become friends and form playgroups most readily with those who share their demographic characteristics. The same kind of self-segregation can be seen on a college campus or in the cafeteria of any large corporation. A preference for working with those of the same "race and ethnicity creates the strongest divides in our personal environments, with age, religion, education, occupation, and gender following in roughly that order," states one study.

When nearly 100 pairs of twins were put in the same kind of partner's dilemma as used in Robert Axelrod's computer tournament, identical twins, genetic copies of each other, collaborated much better than fraternal twins, who are no more genetically alike than any other pair of brothers or sisters. One Canadian researcher tricked her subjects by digitally morphing their own photos with those of strangers and presenting the results as the faces of people with whom the volunteer was playing a game of trust. People trusted the "self-morphs" more than photos created from the images of two strangers. (Another study even found that when people adopt a purebred puppy, they tend to choose dogs that look like themselves.)

Sociologists call the degree of similarity between people "social distance." Its consequences for collaboration are often more important than the physical distance separating two counterparts. Humans are tribal creatures, constantly drawing boundaries — sometimes prejudicial boundaries — between friends and foes.

This creates a problem, not only because it restricts your collaborative field, but because it makes you less likely to create strong ties with those who would bring something you lack to the partnership. Many of the potential collaborators you need most are those who will be, because of their differences from you, most difficult to learn to accept. You don't need an identical twin as much as you need an opposite, a relative stranger who shares the common mission and the same sense of fair play, but whose approach to the challenge may seem quite foreign.

The most successful partnerships bridge this gap. In addition to agreeing with the complementary strengths statements in Chapter One, effective allies most strongly agree with three statements regarding acceptance that emerged from Gallup's structured interviews:

- We focus on each other's strengths, not weaknesses.

- We accept each other as we are and don't try to change each other.

- We are understanding of each other when one of us makes mistakes.

Eighty-three percent of those in a good partnership agree with the second statement, but only 16 percent in poor working relationships do so. The most effective pairs are also far more likely to agree with the other two statements. As with the other elements of collaboration, only those who strongly agree to all three statements can be said to have an excellent partnership.

Differences between partners can easily spark antagonism. One man shared his frustrations in dealing with a fellow parishioner in his late teens when they were teamed up to prepare the music for a Sunday morning worship service. "Practice was a nightmare," he said. "I think we both felt the other was attacking when pointing out something that needed to be changed. There was also a generation gap. I was 'old and outdated' in his eyes, and I struggled with some of the off-the-wall ideas he had. We ended up fighting over whether or not to play a certain chord somewhere and what order to play the songs in. Everything said was met with defensiveness and said with a semi-joking, passive-aggressive attitude. I haven't worked with this person since, and I would avoid doing so in the future."

Even if the social distance between you and your partner is small, incorporating his or her personality into your preferred way of working can be difficult. Mutual irritation is common in partnerships, particularly in the early stages. There is a natural propensity to believe you are normal and that the other person, to the degree she differs from you, is a bit off.

Psychologists call it egocentrism. We tend to forget or disregard information that disagrees with us, but we remember what reinforces our own views. We are inclined to believe positive news about those we like and negative information about those we don't. We suffer the hubris of "egocentric infallibility," thinking what we believe must be true because we would not believe something unless it were true. And we are hypocrites, believing or professing one thing and doing another, sometimes not even noticing the contradiction in ourselves while having a finely honed sense for spotting it in others.

"Egocentric thinking emerges from our innate human tendency to see the world from a narrow, self-serving perspective," wrote one pair of experts on human thinking. "We naturally think of the world in terms of how it can serve us. Our instinct is to continually operate within the world, to manipulate situations and people, in accordance with our selfish interests."

Egocentrism kills partnerships. It's impossible to work effectively with someone if you, blind to your own failings, spend too much energy finding fault with your comrade. Partnerships require both people to accommodate each other's foibles. "The cockpit can be a small place, especially when laboring with someone who has a different philosophical bent or focus on details," said one captain for a major American airline. "As we sometimes say to friends when flying with those free spirits, 'We are on Day 12 of a five-day trip.'"

Warren Murphy, author of dozens of mysteries and one of the scriptwriters for the film *Lethal Weapon 2*, had three words of advice for authors who are thinking of teaming up with another writer: "Don't. Don't. Don't."

"You think a puppy's trouble? Wait until you get somebody who goes angsting around, all aquiver with outraged indignation over the deletion of a comma," he warned. "One of the real problems with partnering is all the time you waste trying not to hurt your partner's feelings, and in the end, it won't do you a bit of good because your partner knows you are a crass, unfeeling egomaniac interested only in yourself. And wait until you are forced to spend time with someone who hates you because, walking into a room together, six people know your name and only five in the room know your partner's. Clearly you have been up to something criminous at his expense."

"And the writing itself," he continues. "Two months into the partnership and you will wonder how you ever managed to get yourself saddled with a logically challenged half-wit who is functionally illiterate to boot. Your partner, meanwhile, thinks exactly the same thing but blames it on your Alzheimer's and sends you a box of Depends on your birthday . . . just in case."

If you can't find a way to accept your counterpart's personality, the parishioner, the pilot, and Murphy are right. The Christmas program will be torture, the flights too long, and coauthoring the book a huge chore. You can easily justify finding fault with your counterpart because every one of his or her strengths can be upended and seen as a weakness. A colleague who excels in generating ideas will of course be less practical, because thinking outside the box starts with ignoring the box. Someone who takes command can be viewed as bossy. A partner who carefully assesses the risks can be tagged as "chicken."

Just as a hammer makes a poor saw and pliers make a poor paintbrush, any strength can be faulted for its failings, and any person can be criticized for what she does not do well. To the degree that you insist on taking the negative view of your collaborator's personality, you will destroy the partnership.

ALL HIS LIFE, VIVIEN THOMAS wanted to be a doctor. But in 1930, the aspiring black 19-year-old saw his savings from seven years of carpentry work, his hopes of attending college, and his "trust in everything and everybody" evaporate when the bank where he kept those savings folded.

At the time, he had been working only a few months for Alfred Blalock, a white 31-year-old Vanderbilt University Hospital physician trying to come back from his own setback of not having received a surgical residency at Johns Hopkins, where he attended medical school. Blalock was in charge of the research lab at Vanderbilt, and he hired Thomas to assist him in conducting experiments.

Blalock was highly driven, inclined to take on as much as possible. Even as a boy, he was unwilling to go to bed until his homework was done to his satisfaction. He would cry if he was forced to go to bed before he memorized all his spelling words. A friend warned Thomas about Blalock; he "understood the guy was 'hell' to get along with and didn't think I'd be able to work with him." Needing the job, Thomas applied anyway. He found Blalock, at their first meeting, to be easygoing, quiet, and serious. "I want someone in the laboratory whom I can teach to do anything

I can do and maybe do things I can't do," the doctor told his new hire.

Thomas quickly became proficient at conducting the research, performing experiments on anesthetized dogs and carefully documenting their physiological reactions to trauma and shock in hopes the discoveries could save human lives. At that time, surgeons lost more patients to shock than to any other single cause.

Everything went along fine for a couple months. "We had settled down to what I considered a good working relationship," wrote Thomas. "Then one morning it happened. Something went wrong, I no longer recall what, but I made some error. Dr. Blalock sounded off like a child throwing a temper tantrum. The profanity he used would have made the proverbial sailor proud of him." Blalock retrieved a Coke from the lab's walk-in refrigerator and stormed off, leaving Thomas to wonder what had just happened, and why. The technician changed out of his lab clothes and went into Blalock's office. The doctor looked surprised, as if nothing happened.

"I told him he could just pay me off, that I was trying but that if it was going to be like this every time I made a mistake, and I couldn't please him, my staying around would only cause trouble," wrote Thomas. Blalock apologized. He said he lost his temper and that it would never happen again. He asked Thomas to return to work, which he did. Thomas resolved to quit if Blalock lost his cool again, as one of the other men in the lab assured him it would.

"But Dr. Blalock kept his word for the next 34 years, even though I made mistakes," wrote Thomas. "We had occasional disagreements and sometimes even heated discussions. But neither of us ever hesitated to let the other know, in a straightforward man-to-man manner, what he thought or how he felt, whether it concerned research or, in later years, the administration of the laboratory. In retrospect, I think this incident set the stage for what I consider our mutual respect throughout the years."

Blalock and Thomas' partnership was far from perfect. Given the disparity in their education and status and their different races in a time of segregation, they did not receive equal acclaim or pay for work they largely shared. Throughout their collaboration, it was clear Blalock was in charge, with Thomas following. Inside the lab, however, they came to treat each other as partners in a way that was remarkable for the time.

For all their differences, Blalock and Thomas shared important similarities. Both were trying to redeem themselves of their own unmet expectations. Both were intensely hard workers and dedicated to the practice of medicine. Both were highly skilled practitioners, although in different and complementary ways. As the doctor became increasingly busy outside the lab, Thomas took on more responsibility. Soon he was not just preparing the animals for surgery, but conducting the complete operation.

In 1940, Blalock was offered a job as surgeon-in-chief and chairman of the department of surgery at Johns

Hopkins, the institution that left him so disappointed earlier in his life. He was getting his career back on track. "If I accept it, and I'm sure I will, I want you to go with me," the doctor told his associate. Blalock accepted the post, and both men moved themselves and their families to Baltimore.

People at Hopkins were surprised at the degree of autonomy Thomas had. Their reaction got him thinking about his abilities and his relationship to Blalock. The other lab staff "had never heard of a surgical research technician doing what I was doing. Certainly none of the technicians at Hopkins did the work I did," wrote Thomas. "Was my position an invention of Blalock? Was I someone he could teach to do the things he could do and maybe do things he could not do? Surely I was no robot. At what other institution would I be able to find individuals without academic degrees who would fall into my category?"

Blalock left little record of his thoughts about the collaboration. It is apparent, however, that the two men came to accept — as effective partners must — the unique, potentially grating characteristics of the other. Having drawn the line at severe and profane eruptions, Thomas nonetheless had to accept that Blalock was generally reserved and unsympathetic.

"In the operating room, Dr. Blalock was tense and impatient and, as a result, the atmosphere became tense the moment he entered," wrote Thomas. "Even when things were progressing smoothly he would find something to complain about. Complaining seems to be a part of him. No one ever seemed to give him sufficient assistance." This intensity made many of the staff nervous and less effective. But Thomas, knowing how deeply Blalock cared about the patients and about doing a good job, learned to deal with it. "To me," he said, "this seemed to be his method of venting some of the pressure he was feeling."

Thomas had to accept that Blalock involved himself in so much that he was often late for experiments, sometimes not showing up at all. While this confused Thomas early in their partnership, the necessity of proceeding without the doctor gave the technician greater latitude to demonstrate his abilities. "One should never try to picture the professor [Blalock] as a saint or a god; one of his chief virtues is his 'earthly human shortcomings,' faults that color his character and give it a spark and interest that so many men in comparable positions fail to have," wrote one of his colleagues in 1964.

A creature of his time, Blalock was not opposed to segregation nor struck by the irony of allowing his collaborator to moonlight as a bartender at parties he hosted. It is difficult to know what part of his imperial bearing at the beginning of the partnership was because of race and what stemmed from the traditional doctor-staff hierarchy that continues in hospitals today. Ultimately, the surgeon had to adjust his thinking about Thomas to accommodate the technician's genius. Blalock almost certainly did not anticipate that a black man with only a high school education would be the most important collaborator in his career. But as Thomas stood up for himself and showed his abilities, Blalock found ways to increase Thomas' pay, sought and valued his opinions, coauthored papers with him, and accepted job offers only if his technician also received employment in the deal.

While the disparities in rank and prestige remained, the collaboration itself became increasingly equal. In surgeries on animals, they sometimes reversed roles, with Thomas operating and Blalock assisting. "It was extremely difficult to tell if Dr. Blalock had the original idea for a particular technique or if it was Vivien Thomas, they worked so well together," observed another Hopkins surgeon.

When Dr. Helen Taussig approached Blalock about the "blue babies" (children with a particular congenital heart defect) under her care, Blalock asked Thomas to join him and Taussig to discuss the possibilities. Thomas spent hours examining the preserved hearts of children who had died of the malady, looking for a way to essentially re-plumb the organ. He found a way to replicate the problem in dogs so he could then experiment with possible surgical solutions. He modified surgical instruments to fit the new procedure. Having done many surgeries on the dogs, Thomas trained Blalock on the procedure.

In November of 1944, a surgical team was mobilized to conduct the first of these operations on a little girl named Eileen Saxon who was so critically ill that without the operation, she was almost certain to die. Thomas helped with the preparations but stayed behind during the surgery, afraid his presence would make Blalock nervous. With everything in place and before proceeding, the surgeon turned to his already scrubbed and gowned chemistry technician and said, "I'd guess you'd better go call Vivien."

Thomas went to the gallery overlooking the operating room. "Vivien, you'd better come down here," said Blalock, positioning Thomas where he could best observe the procedure and consult with the doctor, looking over Blalock's right shoulder. Blalock asked Thomas if the transverse incision was long enough. Yes, he said, if not too long. The two men collaborated throughout the operation.

After an hour and a half of surgery, the clamps were finally removed. The sutures held. Taussig, standing at the head of the operating table, turned to Blalock and said, "Al, the baby's lips are a glorious pink color."

Having accomplished the first blue baby operation, Blalock and Thomas continued their work, refining the instruments and the procedure. Many times, Blalock called for Thomas to resume his place at his right shoulder. If anyone else moved into that spot, he would tell them, "Only Vivien is to stand there."

Blalock's dependence on the man he called "my superb technician," his near-pleading that Thomas stay with him throughout his medical career, and his respectful treatment of him in a era when blacks were poorly regarded suggest Blalock more than anyone knew the value of the partnership.

Through his work with the doctor, Thomas went on to become an instructor to medical students at Johns Hopkins. He was awarded an honorary doctorate by the institution. When it came time to decide where to put a painting of Thomas, the school announced, "We are going to hang your fine portrait with Professor Blalock. We think you 'hung' together and you had better continue to hang together."

Even if he had attended medical school, Thomas would have had difficulty making a larger mark on medicine than he did with the surgeon he came to accept as his partner.

STRONG PARTNERSHIPS DON'T JUST FALL INTO PLACE when one great person happens upon another whose personality is ideal. Every collaboration is a combination of two imperfect creatures. One of the greatest challenges of any partnership is learning how to work in close quarters with another over-assuming, fallible, emotionally driven, partially informed, idiosyncratic being moving up and down on the tides of life just like you. The most successful partners come to accept the rough edges of their colleagues. The best collaborators understand they are no more going to get a perfect partner than they are going to be one, and they make accommodations for each other's human failings.

This element of partnership does not require you to tolerate every kind of behavior. Certain traits or habits are out of bounds. Just as Vivien Thomas refused to be berated by Alfred Blalock, no collaborator should feel an obligation to endure abuse, sloth, dishonesty, selfishness, or a partner taking sole credit for joint accomplishments.

Beyond the universally intolerable acts, you must decide what quirks you personally cannot accept. Liv Arnesen, for example, saw little chance of working with a "publicity hound," "a chatter-box," or someone not prepared for the rigors of the expedition. Many people cannot abide a collaborator with an oversized ego, while some can. The tendency some people have for working right up until a deadline causes some partners great stress, while others find it invigorating.

Be careful about making your list of unacceptable traits too long. As the inventory of behaviors you won't tolerate grows, it begins to say less about the frustrating counterparts with whom you've been paired and more about you being a difficult partner. Having too many conditions can rule out all your potential collaborators. If a particular attribute of your counterpart is not demonstrably wrong, it bears at least an attempt at accommodating. Thomas learned to live with Blalock's intensity and complaining in the operating room. Frank Wells accepted many of Michael Eisner's shortcomings. Liv Arnesen and Ann Bancroft managed to get along well in conditions that drove other polar partnerships to mutual acrimony.

Salt Lake Tribune reporter Michael C. Lewis saw the acceptance grow between Utah Jazz players John Stockton and Karl Malone. "Karl has a very fragile ego," said Lewis. "I think he really very much loved being the guy, being Karl, and being the center of attention. But at the same time, he could manufacture the weirdest ways to be offended or mad. A lot of times they manifested themselves in really maddening ways like a new contract demand or a distracting rant in the press."

Meanwhile, Stockton was at the other extreme, legendary for keeping his emotions to himself. "Karl's almost adolescent sense of self-esteem and egotism, I think, drove John nuts," the journalist speculated. And yet, Stockton never voiced his irritation publicly. "I never heard him say an ill word about him. I got the feeling that John approached it as, 'You know, that's just Karl.' You kind of have to cope with it for the sake of having such a good player around you."

Collaborators look for ways to handle aspects of their opposites they would prefer to change. One is denial, pretending the problem does not exist. Ignoring the issue, according to psychological research, is a poor strategy that has shown itself to be "clearly related to higher levels of stress and impaired psychological well-being." If your partner does something that bothers you, you need to recognize it before you can resolve it.

Another tactic is called "resigning acceptance." This attitude, although it recognizes the problem, also includes a feeling of cynicism or powerlessness in dealing with the issue. "Typical," say people who use this method. "These things always happen to me." Or they may say something such as, "All my practice was for nothing. I did not need to do it at all."

"Resigning acceptance," wrote one group of researchers, "means abandoning outward-directed actions; however, this behavior is combined with negative expectations about the future and a loss of hope." This kind of approach is much like denial, leading to bitterness, decreased mental health, and less control over your actions.

The best way to deal with a frustrating situation is called "active acceptance," neither denying the situation nor surrendering to it. "Active acceptance means acknowledging a negative, difficult situation and dealing with it in a constructive way," wrote the researchers. "The individual dispenses with fruitless attempts to control what is neither controllable nor changeable." Active acceptance is associated with higher levels of happiness and sense of control. In a partnership, it is epitomized by focusing on your partner's strengths rather than her weaknesses, accepting her as she is, and being understanding when she errs. In the best collaborations, partners come to appreciate what they once found aggravating.

A similar phenomenon occurs with social distance. As consistently as one set of experiments shows that demographic differences between players make them less trusting of each other in the early rounds, another set of experiments just as consistently shows that the more two counterparts get to know each other, the better they coordinate their moves. The silver lining of human tribal boundaries is that they are fluid. Spend enough time working shoulder to shoulder with one of "them," and she will become one of "us." We can adopt into our tribe people who are quite different from us. Familiarity eventually trumps dissimilarity. "People come to the table with prejudices and stereotypes," one pair of professors observed. "However, after meeting someone and gaining more information, these prejudices are often revised or washed away."

Even Murphy, the curmudgeonly mystery writer who argued against writing with someone else, formed a strong partnership by ignoring his own advice. He and coauthor Richard Ben Sapir learned to deal with each other. One rewrote the other's work without telling him. One wrecked the other's car. They wrangled over money. They passed manuscripts back and forth on opposing sleep cycles. "We wrote and sold a lot of books, but partnership was different for us and, for the record, none of the things I just complained about [regarding partnerships] had anything to do with me and Richard Ben Sapir."

"He had only one speed: overdrive," wrote Murphy. "He never saved anything for later; he gave you his best work every day. Drunk, sober, happy, sad — none of it mattered. The pages flew from his typewriter."

Ultimately, Murphy was compelled by his own experience to concede that perhaps a collaboration could succeed. Sapir, said the skeptic of partnerships, was "the greatest partner anyone could have."

Chapter Six

Forgiveness

*"He that studieth revenge keepeth his own wounds
green, which otherwise would heal and do well."*

— John Milton

EDWARD R. MURROW AND WILLIAM L. SHIRER needed
to work out a truce.

As correspondents for CBS Radio, they had been the
best of collaborators. They accomplished groundbreaking
broadcasts from pre-war Europe, most famously the first
"European News Roundup," broadcast shortly after the
annexation of Austria by Nazi Germany. It was a journalistic
and technical innovation to get voices from London,
Vienna, Berlin, Paris, and Rome transmitted by shortwave
to the United States. Shirer, one of the only American
broadcasters in Vienna during the *Anschluss*, switched places
with Murrow in London so he could broadcast his account
without censorship.

Collaborating well under such pressure built tremendous
trust between the two reporters. "We have worked together

very closely, Ed and I, during the last three turbulent years over here," wrote Shirer after their last broadcast from Europe, "and a bond grew that was very real, a kind you make only a few times in your life."

In 1947, Shirer was a commentator for CBS. But when the advertiser that sponsored his show grew dissatisfied with him, he was demoted to an unsponsored time slot. Shirer announced his resignation over the air, complaining that a "soap company can decide who cannot be on the air." By going public, Shirer put Murrow, then a CBS executive, in the difficult spot of having to defend the integrity of the network against protestors who were siding with Shirer.

The two men met in the bar of a New York hotel to talk. "They were two old comrades with too much time spent together in the trenches to let it end this way," wrote Murrow biographer Joseph E. Persico. "They agreed that both of them had been pressured into foolish postures." The journalists worked out an arrangement to keep Shirer at CBS. They went to Murrow's office and wrote a statement to give to the press. The men took it to CBS Chief Executive William S. Paley for his approval. "Bill, we have an agreement," said Murrow.

Paley didn't care. "As far as I'm concerned," he told Shirer, "your usefulness has ended. You're out."

Shirer looked to Murrow for support. Instead of backing his longtime ally, Murrow said, "We had an agreement. But if you don't like it, Bill, you're the boss." Shirer felt completely betrayed.

Leaving CBS may ultimately have helped Shirer. Being off the air created the writing obsession that led to Shirer's greatest work, his book *The Rise and Fall of the Third Reich*. "Had Mr. Shirer been broadcasting instead of researching and writing," noted *The New York Times*, "that instructive book might never have come into existence." And Shirer had, after all, resigned on the air. It didn't matter; Murrow had lost Shirer's trust and ignited his indignation. In his 1954 novel, *Stranger Come Home*, Shirer made one of the characters particularly spineless and hypocritical. It was a thinly veiled caricature of Murrow.

Nearly two decades after the incident, Murrow, dying of cancer, requested to see Shirer. The two former allies drove around on a hot summer day near Murrow's farm in upstate New York, Murrow sweating and coughing. "Once or twice he would try to bring up the past, but I would change the subject," recalled Shirer. "I did not want to talk about it. It had happened. It had threatened to destroy me, but I had survived. That was that." They returned to Murrow's house and parted ways. Murrow died the next spring.

"Bill Shirer had tried to cut the memory out of his heart," wrote Persico, "and forgiveness had gone with it."

When a partnership is going well, all kinds of wonderfully unselfish things happen. Partners change their goals to better match each other's objectives. They strive to be fair to each other. They focus on their counterparts' strengths. They overlook each other's foibles. At the zenith of collaboration, both partners make great personal sacrifices for the other's happiness.

But when things turn negative, a parallel set of emotions and reactions kicks in. The partners see themselves as pursuing opposing ends. Fairness becomes less about a considerate division of rewards and work and more about what one partner feels the other owes her. The counterpart's strengths don't seem so impressive any more. His personal ticks become full-fledged character flaws. At the nadir of collaboration, not only will the partners refuse to sacrifice for each other's benefit, they eagerly go out of their way to cause their one-time comrade pain.

"There will be a day of reckoning," Terry Garnett told himself when Oracle CEO Larry Ellison fired him. Garnett eventually became chairman of Ingres, a competitor of Oracle. "I do hold grudges," Garnett told *BusinessWeek*. "Am I motivated by that? Absolutely."

The same emotional wiring that makes great partnerships so effective and rewarding creates corresponding and equally powerful negative forces if things go wrong. In a good collaboration, partners make statements such as "two heads are better than one." In a bad one, the two make comments such as "I would have been better off working by myself" or "I wish I'd never even met him."

Two statements in Gallup's research differentiate good and bad partnerships on keeping the collaboration from going negative:

- There have been times when either my collaborator or I have violated the other's trust.

- When either of us has violated the other's trust, we have been able to forgive each other.

Although minor disruptions occur in good and bad partnerships, serious violations of trust are rare in the best pairs. Only 18 percent of good partnerships suffer a real rift. Among poor partnerships, the number jumps to 40 percent.

If such a breach occurs, those in a good partnership are better at working through it. When something serious enough to require forgiveness transpires, 85 percent of those in good partnerships do forgive. Those in poor partnerships patch things up only 14 percent of the time.

Trust between two collaborators is like the rope between mountaineers on a snowy ledge. If the line is cut, the gravity of powerful negative emotions kicks in. The cord may have been separated one fiber at a time, as when a snide remark, showing up late for an important meeting, or letting a shared project slide a little leads to a matching dereliction from the other guy. Or it may have been sliced in two with one stroke, as Shirer felt it had when Murrow failed to back him up. In either case, the former collaborators become subject to an "irrational" desire to return wrong for wrong.

Revenge is sweet. One brain-imaging study found that the enjoyment of striking back is processed in the same part of the brain that recognizes the pleasure of eating chocolate. The sweetest retaliation is more than a symbolic protest; it punishes the offender. Although the victim of the original offense gets nothing from the revenge except the satisfaction of seeing the other guy hurt, experiments have demonstrated that he is more than willing to pay to extract a cost from the other guy. Getting even can be as rewarding as reaching a major goal with someone else, making retribution a tempting alternative to collaboration.

Why would such a negative force be so powerful? Evolutionary psychologists think it stems from the need to maintain order in primitive societies. "For thousands of years, human societies did not have the modern institutions of law enforcement — impartial police and impartial judges that ensure the punishment of norm violations such as cheating in an economic exchange," noted one set of scholars. "Social norms had to be enforced by other measures, and private sanctions were one of these means." One economist even went so far as to call our willingness to punish bad guys "the cement of society."

We rarely admit how much we enjoy revenge. Something in our upbringing tells us it's not right to feel that way, even though we do. But the evidence is all around. Think of how many action movies you've seen in which the emotional payoff at the end is seeing the bad guy get what's coming to him. "The powerful appeal of the revenge theme in mass entertainment," wrote one commentator, "is simply one more manifestation of the gap between private feelings about revenge and the public pretense that justice and vengeance have nothing, perish the uncivilized thought, to do with each other."

In the movies, villains get impaled (*Lethal Weapon 4*), are forced out the back of an airborne plane (*Air Force One*), or get shot reaching for their guns (*Dirty Harry*). In real life, they suffer less violent but equally deserving fates.

"Every time we were to meet with the CEO to present our recommendations, my boss would have me do the report and then he would put a new cover sheet on the report with his name as the author," one volunteer told a group of researchers studying revenge. "Then, at the meeting, he would refer all of the CEO's questions to me while taking all of the credit for the report. So, one day, I had finally had it. I did the report as requested. But on the day of the presentation to the CEO, I took a 'holiday' from work. At that meeting, the CEO asked my boss the questions and he could not answer any of them. The CEO investigated and my boss was fired. I was promoted to my boss' position."

The human mind admires a good payback. "Poetic justice" occurs when it serves a larger purpose than just repaying harm inflicted on the victim, when it's ingenious, and when it makes the offender the instrument of his own demise. "Revenge may be more aesthetically pleasing when it is not simply a repetition of the provocation," wrote the scientists who reported the bad boss story. "To truly 'one-up' the harmdoer and impress others, the avenger may have to demonstrate some originality and creativity."

Just as Shirer mocked Murrow in his novel, Michelangelo painted his critic, Vatican Master of Ceremonies Biagio da Cesena, into the Sistine Chapel, making him Minos, judge of the underworld with a large snake curled around his legs as he watches the damned arrive in Hell. It's widely believed Jeffrey Katzenberg — of whom Disney CEO Michael Eisner once said, "I think I hate the little midget" — modeled "pushy, vain and real-estate hungry" Lord Farquaad, the villain of the movie *Shrek*, after his former boss.

The vicarious satisfaction, the smirk we get from hearing how the plagiarizing manager was exposed or how a former Disney CEO was mocked in, of all things, a children's movie only serves to demonstrate the real temptation of what scientists call "negative reciprocity" — and its danger. The retaliation reflex may be "the cement of society," but it fractures partnerships. Vengeful feelings quickly get out of hand. Animosity can simmer for years. "A central problem in escalating feuds is that both parties use different arithmetics to calculate the balance," wrote the poetic justice researchers.

One of the most difficult collaborative decisions you will face is whether to patch up a partnership if your counterpart violates your trust. There is no perfect answer. Anyone who tells you to just let it go is failing to consider the intensity of his own emotions under these circumstances. Problems serious enough to require wrestling with the decision are sparked by offenses that would justify writing off your partner.

Yet failing to continue working together can forfeit the benefits of what was otherwise a solid combination. "Some of these relationships are too good to destroy just because somebody harms us," said Michael E. McCullough, an expert on the psychology of revenge and forgiveness. "We have to have a way of getting over the fact that we're going to get into squabbles [and] we're going to have conflicts of interest. Not only in the human species, but in non-human primates, you see evidence that when they harm each other they really are predisposed to try to patch those relationships back together."

Common sense (confirmed in the research) indicates what needs to be done by the offender: Apologize. Make your good intentions clear. Make a peace offering. Be demonstrably more reliable to rebuild trust.

The more intriguing question is what to do if you were the one betrayed. You need a tremendous amount of discernment, self-control, ability to give your counterpart the benefit of the doubt, and desire for a better outcome to turn a vicious circle into a virtuous one. How you manage your own thinking is as important as the offense itself. In many cases, whether a person forgives the misdeed says less about the seriousness of the wrong than about the personality of the partner whose trust was abused.

According to conventional wisdom that dates back as far as Aristotle, feelings of anger need to be vented or released to avoid having them build up to a much larger explosion. Sigmund Freud argued that if people didn't react forcefully to an emotional offense, they would continue to carry unresolved feelings. "Language attests to this fact of daily observation in such expressions as 'to give vent to one's feeling,' to be 'relieved by weeping,' etc.," he wrote. "If the reaction is suppressed, the affect remains united with the memory. An insult retaliated, be it only in words, is differently recalled than one that had to be taken in silence . . . the reaction of an injured person to a trauma has really only then a perfect 'cathartic' effect if it is expressed in an adequate reaction like revenge."

Freud's advice has been repeated over the subsequent decades. "Punch a pillow or a punching bag. Punch with all the frenzy you can," states a 1993 book on anger management. "If you are angry at a particular person, imagine his or her face on the pillow or punching bag, and vent your rage physically and verbally. You will be doing violence to a pillow or punching bag so that you can stop doing violence to yourself by holding in poisonous anger."

There's just one problem with this strategy: It doesn't work. By Freud's theory, if someone who was insulted by a colleague were to divert his anger into pounding nails for 10 minutes, he should have gotten much of the frustration out of his system. In 1959, a University of Iowa researcher tested this idea, allowing half his subjects the chance to hammer out their anger over such an insult. Then he observed as each of the volunteers got the chance to criticize the original offender. Those who spent time hammering nails were more, not less, hostile toward the person who insulted them.

In 2002, a professor at Iowa State University had hundreds of students write a brief political essay. He told them another student would comment on what they wrote, when in fact he had already prepared scathing reviews. He slammed the essays on their organization, originality, writing style, clarity, persuasiveness, and overall quality. On a scale ranging from -10 (very bad) to +10 (very good), every essay got a score between -8 and -10. He also attached a handwritten comment to each essay that read: "This is one of the worst essays I have read!" ("Previous research has shown that this procedure makes people quite angry," the professor added.)

Some of the students were given boxing gloves and a 70-pound punching bag. They were instructed to hit it as much as they wanted while thinking of the person who criticized their essays. A picture of the purported offender's face was shown on a computer monitor. Others were made to just sit, waiting while the experimenter pretended to be fixing their partner's computer. Hitting the punching bag not only failed to alleviate anger and aggression, it increased the negative feelings.

"The results from the present research show that venting to reduce anger is like using gasoline to put out a fire — it only feeds the flame," wrote the professor. "By fueling aggressive thoughts and feelings, venting also increases aggressive responding. People who walloped the punching bag while thinking about the person who had provoked them were the most angry and the most aggressive."

Taken together, a number of recent studies indicate that the more one entertains the anger or recalls the bad event, the less likely it is to be resolved, and therefore the less likely the partnership will survive the rift. What the academic journals call "rumination," what you probably call "stewing" or "fuming," only makes things worse.

So what should you do to get over a rough patch in your partnership? The most constructive strategies require you to find a middle ground between being aloof and submersing yourself in the emotions triggered by the event — close enough to work through the situation, far enough to avoid reliving it. Those who find this middle ground are able to evaluate the reasons why they got upset without stirring up the original emotions.

One of the best ways to resolve a past problem is to find the positive in it. Shirer would have been better off thinking less about Murrow's refusal to back him and more about how his break from CBS led him to write his best book. With his success in his new partnerships, Katzenberg is philosophical about his time with Eisner. "I had 10 great years at Disney," he told a reporter in 2007. "I worked for Michael for 19 years and did very, very well with him. I don't even have any bad feelings. I don't feel any resentment. Nothing."

A study of 304 students who were asked to recall "a harmful thing that someone you know did to you" found that the students who were instructed to think about the upside did much better working through it. "We would like for you to write about *positive* aspects of the experience," the researchers told the volunteers. "In which ways did the thing that this person did to you lead to positive consequences for you? Perhaps you became aware of personal strengths that you did not realize you had, perhaps a relationship became better or stronger as a result, or perhaps you grew or became a stronger or wiser person."

The students who were given this assignment found the task "remarkably easy to complete," wrote the professors. They listed benefits such as discovering a previously unknown strength, becoming wiser and better at communicating, increased confidence, learning forgiveness, and even strengthening their relationship with the person who first aggravated them. The students who looked for benefits were more forgiving — less vengeful and less likely to avoid the offender — than other volunteers who were instructed to dwell on the offense itself in their writing.

Nonetheless, it takes a rare level of maturity and self-awareness to let the trespass pass. "In a former workplace I had a chance to undermine a coworker who'd previously earned my dislike," one reader wrote to *BusinessWeek* after the publication of a cover article on revenge. "Due to a computer malfunction, a 100-page document she was composing vanished. The loss guaranteed she'd never make her deadline. I watched her stress mount for a moment or two, but I couldn't resist pointing out something she didn't know. She'd accidentally cc'd me a recent draft of her document. Relief washed over her as she realized she'd make her deadline after all."

"Why did I do that?" the writer asked himself. "I guess having whiffed the dregs of retribution, I realized something George Orwell once wrote: 'Revenge is sour.'"

★★

It took John Adams and Thomas Jefferson nearly until the ends of their lives to accomplish the reconciliation that eluded Shirer and Murrow. But once the men began their reconciliation, they made it a fitting bookend to the historic accomplishments that began their work together.

The two delegates to the Continental Congress were legendary collaborators on the Declaration of Independence; Jefferson was its author and Adams its leading defender in the new legislature. They were highly successful diplomatic partners representing the new country to England and France. But they created an often intense rivalry as president and vice president, and they ceased communicating for more than a decade.

As the men became older, they were at risk of not patching up their relationship before one of them passed away. Then on New Year's Day of 1812, at the urging of mutual friends, the 76-year-old Adams wrote the letter that reestablished their partnership. He sent along some writings of his son, John Quincy Adams, certainly knowing it would tug at Jefferson's heartstrings. "I wish you, sir, many happy New Years and that you may enter the next and many succeeding years with as animating prospects for the public as those at present before us." It was a short letter, but as a signal of trust, it was enough to bridge the distance.

Jefferson reciprocated at length. "A letter from you calls up recollections very dear to my mind," replied the 68-year-old Virginian. "It carries me back to the times when, beset with difficulties and dangers, we were fellow laborers in the same cause, struggling for what is most valuable to man, his right of self-government." He closed the letter by assuring Adams that nothing had "suspended for one moment my sincere esteem for you: and I now salute you with unchanged affections and respect."

The initial exchange began a 14-year correspondence between the former presidents. They exchanged theories on the origin of Native Americans, opinions on being liberated from English dictionaries to develop an American dialect, and their separate views on social equality. They argued. They made little apologies and modest concessions. They rebuilt the trust that they could disagree without threatening the bond between them. "You and I ought not to die before we have explained ourselves to each other," wrote Adams in July 1813.

And so they did, exchanging 161 letters between them after reestablishing communication. What started as the renewal of a friendship between the two men evolved into a form of long-distance collaboration as the writing they exchanged began to accumulate into a considerable collection. In effect, they were writing their own histories and doing it together. "Both men," observed historian Joseph

J. Ellis, "knew they were sending their letters to posterity as much as to each other."

Just as their partnership began by collaborating on one of America's most important historical documents, their work culminated in the creation of a vital record of two founding fathers. While their letters include news of their personal lives and the typical greetings one person sends another through the mail, they also include bits of debate, brief editorials, scientific and religious musings, and explanations of their respective rationales sprinkled with idioms and wit. Their letters make the patriots not the marble statues chiseled by the passage of time, but flesh-and-blood collaborators whose struggles can be appreciated by partners today.

The Adams-Jefferson letters present one of the best illustrations of a partnership reconciled and returned to action. They exhibit the two men's passion for the mission that first united them — the independence and success of the United States.

Adams had enough confidence in Jefferson not to be offended when, over the course of their writing, the Virginian wrote only one letter to every two from the Massachusetts lawyer. "Never mind . . . if I write four letters to your one," wrote Adams. "Your one is worth more than my four." The correspondence shows a high degree of appreciation for the other's abilities, acceptance of each other's uniqueness, and concerns for the counterpart's happiness. The letters reveal the men in their last years to be fundamentally the same people they were when younger — Adams, for example, seeking to provoke a debate and Jefferson tactfully dodging it.

The letters even demonstrate an interest in how history would judge the other person. "If your objects and opinions have been misunderstood, if the measures and principles of others have wrongly been imputed to you, as I believe they have been, that you should leave an explanation of them, would be an act of justice to yourself," Jefferson wrote to Adams in June of 1813.

Their exchanges are long enough to fill a book. The post-reconciliation writings between the two men are "one of the most extraordinary correspondences in American history — indeed, in the English language," wrote historian David McCullough. "The level and range of their discourse was always above and beyond the ordinary. . . . They were two leading statesmen of the time, but also two of the finest writers, and they were showing what they could do."

Had they not picked up their pens and dropped their grudges, American history would have been poorer. Although they corresponded heavily while diplomats in London and France, half the writing the men exchanged was after their 1812 rapprochement. The collection of letters, wrote Ellis, "is generally regarded as the intellectual capstone to the achievements of the revolutionary generation." The relationship that began in partnership, but split into mutual distrust, ended with another landmark collaboration.

On July 2, 1826, Jefferson became unconscious. He awakened briefly the next evening and asked, "Is it the Fourth?" Told it soon would be, he clung to life until the middle of the following day, exactly 50 years from the date of the Declaration of Independence.

That morning in Quincy, Massachusetts, as a cannon fired in the distance to mark the holiday, Adams also lay dying. Told it was the Fourth, he replied, "It is a great day. It is a *good* day." Later in the afternoon, he spoke again. "Thomas Jefferson survives," he whispered, unaware it was not true. Shortly thereafter, Adams died.

Six years before their nearly simultaneous deaths, with the reconciliation between them complete and the correspondence well underway, Adams was asked by his occasional secretary, Harvard student Josiah Quincy, how he could be on such good terms with someone who had been an adversary. Adams was philosophical. The differences were political, not personal. "He wished to be president of the United States, and I stood in his way," Quincy quoted Adams as saying. "So he did everything that he could to pull me down. But if I should quarrel with him for that, I might quarrel with every man I have had anything to do with in life. And this is human nature . . . I forgive all my enemies and hope they may find a mercy in Heaven. Mr. Jefferson and I have grown old and retired from public life. So we are upon our ancient terms of goodwill."

Chapter Seven

Communicating

★★

"The more elaborate our means of communication,
the less we communicate."

— Joseph Priestley

CAPTAIN KIM SASSE and First Officer Jonathan Palmer got along quite well. "I have a good time flying with you," Palmer told Sasse at the controls of American Connection Flight 5966. "Yeah, me too," said Sasse.

The evening flight on October 19, 2004, was a short one from St. Louis to Adair County, Missouri. Thirteen passengers were on board, most of them medical professionals on their way to a conference. The atmosphere in the cockpit was more than relaxed. "Gotta have fun," said Sasse.

"That's truth, Man. Gotta have the fun," agreed his co-pilot.

"Too many of these [expletive] take themselves way too serious in this job," said the pilot. "I hate it. I've flown with them and it sucks. A month of [expletive] agony . . . All you want to do is strangle the [expletive] when you get on the ground." He broadcast a burp over the radio.

About 23 minutes before they were scheduled to land, the pilots heard an automated weather report from their destination that visibility was poor because of mist and a heavy overcast.

"We're not getting in," said Sasse.

"Go all this [expletive] way," said Palmer. "Well, let's try it."

"Yeah, we'll try it," replied Sasse. "I don't want to go all the way out here for nothing tonight."

The rest of the flight was a mixture of good teamwork between the two pilots and the same kind of joking that occurred earlier. But while casual conversations are allowed at cruising altitude, they are specifically forbidden as the plane is descending to land. Communication is supposed to be strictly business, with specific roles, phrases, and contingencies.

"We're going into the crap," said Sasse as they descended to the top of the clouds in the darkness.

"Look, ooh, it's so eerie and creepy. [I] get a suffocating feeling when I see that." Palmer made a barking sound.

"I'm drowning," joked the captain.

While much of what the two men communicated followed proper procedures — the angle of the flaps, confirming the landing gear was down, conducting the pre-landing checklist — they missed several crucial "callouts." In doing so, they confused their roles and made serious errors.

Palmer failed to announce one of the altitude thresholds and announced another incorrectly. The captain was supposed to be leveling off and monitoring the instruments while the first officer looked for the lights of the airport. Sasse was not supposed to switch from the instruments to visually guiding in the plane unless Palmer announced, "Runway in sight." He never did. The plane was descending too fast, below the minimum altitude that Palmer should have called out to the captain. Palmer failed to challenge Sasse's continued descent.

"I can see ground there," said the pilot.

"I can't see [expletive]," said the co-pilot.

The last communications between Sasse and Palmer were their panicked realizations they were about to hit the ground.

"Trees!" said Palmer.

"No. Stop!" blurted out Sasse.

"Oh my God!" exclaimed the co-pilot.

"Holy [expletive]!"

The airplane smashed into a bean field, broke apart, and burst into flames less than two miles from the airport. Both pilots and 11 of their 13 passengers were killed.

In its report on the accident, the National Transportation Safety Board faulted the pilots for, among other things, not keeping their communications focused enough on the flight and failing to make several crucial "callouts" between them.

Most of the blame was placed on Sasse for not setting the proper tone inside the cockpit. "Had he emphasized the pilots' goals and strategies as they prepared for the [approach and landing], it is likely that the [Flight 5966] pilots would have suspended their humorous banter and engaged in only operationally relevant conversation below 10,000 feet," stated the report.

Poor communication between the pilots cost the lives of 13 people.

MOST COLLABORATORS, even many of the best, do not realize the role communication plays in creating a powerful partnership. Of course two people working together must synchronize their efforts to avoid getting their wires crossed. It's obvious that silence can breed misunderstandings. Of course two heads cannot be better than one if the two people do not talk enough to each other. Everyone gets that.

Rarely appreciated, however, is how communicating itself is collaborative, an issue of trust within the larger partnership that surrounds it. Communication is more than a purely functional aspect of working together. Every time two counterparts talk, their relationship changes. What goes on beneath the surface is more important than the information exchanged.

The three statements about communicating that emerged from Gallup's research demonstrate the importance of more than just both people keeping the other informed about what they are doing:

- We rarely misunderstand each other.
- We are good listeners for each other.
- We show appreciation for what the other does.

On a 1-to-5 scale, people in good partnerships average at least 3.6 on these statements, while excellent collaborators score a perfect 5.0. Anything below 2.0 is poor. The most successful collaborators spend enough time communicating to know what the other is thinking, and they encourage each other along the way. The implied motivations behind the messages are crucial.

Communicating is such a major issue that experiments testing cooperation routinely prohibit the two subjects from talking, sending signals, or even seeing each other. Because the best strategy differs so much depending on whether the other person will prove to be friend or foe, our brains latch onto the slightest cues — smiles, winks, nods, or handshakes — to assess a counterpart's trustworthiness. These little signals "provide a fast and frugal way" to get a collaboration going. According to one theory, the most cooperative people have superior emotional radar for finding others they can trust, but only if they have the chance to communicate.

It's not just the content, it's the contract that only real conversation creates. In one of the few partner's dilemma experiments that let the players interact, volunteers were separated into four groups. In the first group, counterparts could not communicate with each other. The second could send text messages. The third had a computer-generated voice read their messages back and forth. And in the fourth group, the subjects could hold normal telephone conversations. The closer the communication was to normal human speech, the more the two players trusted each other. Almost all of those allowed to talk by phone quickly agreed to transmit all their points to each other every round and maintained that cooperation until near the end of the game.

From a practical perspective, staying in contact with your partner allows the two of you to be aware of the other's next move, to make your intentions clear, to brainstorm or perhaps stumble onto an idea you would not have had separately, and to share your candid assessments with each other.

More important, the communication is as much a form of collaboration as the hands-on work between you and your counterpart. Although it's unlikely you have said these things directly to your collaborator, the underlying messages of your best discussions are: "I'm trusting you with information I don't reveal elsewhere," "You can count on me to do what I say," and "I will look out for you along the way." Plans the two of you make together reinforce the idea that it is a joint project rather than the work of just one or the other.

When the channels are open, communication between you and your collaborator can become a safe testing ground for new ideas — half-baked thoughts you would be uncomfortable sharing with less trusted associates. The ability to "think out loud" with someone who will not scoff, who will try to improve on the idea, and who will keep your confidence is a major advantage two people have over one person working alone. One executive reported that before one of his colleagues would say something risky or confidential, he would preface it by saying he was going "on belay."

"Do you have a policy of checking with each other before you do something big?" an interviewer for *Fortune* magazine asked Dell Chairman Michael Dell and CEO Kevin Rollins at the peak of their success.

"Yeah," they responded in unison.

"When Kevin makes a decision by himself or I make a decision by myself, it's never quite as good as if we make decisions together," said Dell.

Rollins added, "We both sometimes have wacky ideas."

"What's an example of a wacky idea that one of you talked the other out of?" asked the reporter.

"When you have a stupid idea, you don't want to tell everybody," said Rollins.

"At least you were smart enough not to do it," said the journalist.

"That's why we're smart enough not to tell you about it," said Dell.

Silence creates the opposite effects. You won't look stupid if you keep quiet, and you can't be burned with information you never reveal. Suspicious counterparts administer to themselves a sort of mental Miranda warning, worried that anything they say can and will be used against them. But whether or not you intend to do so, failing to communicate creates a threat in your partner's mind that you are not committed to the collaboration, that you do not trust her, or that you just might make a run for the goal by yourself and claim all the credit. It's much easier to vilify someone who has not explained his motivations, much easier to read into the silence the threat of an unpleasant surprise.

When former U.S. President Theodore Roosevelt joined an expedition down Brazil's River of Doubt in 1913, his group was visited one morning by three Nhambiquara Indians. "They left their weapons behind them before they appeared and shouted loudly while they were still hid by the forest," wrote Roosevelt, "and it was only after repeated answering calls of welcome that they approached. Always in the wilderness friends proclaim their presence; a silent advance marks a foe."

The Cuban missile crisis in 1962 not only showed how close the United States and Soviet Union could come to a nuclear war, but also the sorry state of the communication channels needed to avert it. During one point in the crisis, the Soviet ambassador to Washington had to rely on a bicycle courier to take his urgent messages for Moscow to the local Western Union office.

Thereafter, as much as the U.S. and U.S.S.R. were enemies, through better communications, they were also successful partners in keeping the Cold War cold. The two nations agreed to a "Memorandum of Understanding Regarding the Establishment of a Direct Communications Line." Portrayed in movies as red telephones in the White House and Kremlin, the actual, more complicated connection (which connects with the Pentagon, not the White House) was instrumental in allowing both countries to signal each other during the 1967 Arab-Israeli War and avoid the regional conflict becoming a global one. Several other times during the Cold War, the direct connection played a role in keeping either side from doing something that would escalate to conditions neither wanted.

If a direct communications line was so important to two enemies, how much more important is it to two allies?

"I have learned that it always pays to listen to other crew members," one captain for a major U.S. airline told Gallup. "When I initially brief my first officers, I always invite their participation and encourage them to bring forward their experience. I ask them to tell me when I am in error, particularly when I am not in compliance with rules or regulations. We can disagree on politics or religion or investment strategies, but I find it to be a great advantage to harmonize cockpit views regarding our operations. The only way to do that is to respectfully invite and consider first officers' views. God gave them brains, and I would be a fool not to avail myself of their perspectives."

Communication in a partnership is complicated by the unique and incredible human capacity for reading into a situation what the other person must be thinking. If a chimpanzee sees a man holding a banana, the chimp will hold out its hand to beg for the food. If the man has a bucket over his head (as was done in one experiment), the chimp will still hold out its hand. The animal lacks the capacity to perceive the situation from the man's point of view. Any human, even a child, would recognize that the man with the bucket over his head can't see him begging.

Scientists call it recursive thinking, the two- or three-layered awareness of what your collaborator is experiencing. A comment such as "If you're worried that I'm all worked up about it, don't sweat it. We're cool" is loaded with recursion, but partners can untangle this back-and-forth reasoning quite easily. "Recursion," concluded a psychology professor from the University of Auckland, New Zealand, "is a ubiquitous property of the human mind and possibly the principal characteristic that distinguishes our species from all other creatures on the planet."

Recursive thinking is a double-edged sword. There is no sympathy without recursion. A great partner who understands that his colleague is struggling will shoulder more of the burden and offer his support. It's impossible to understand how a collaborator's desire for the goal differs from your own unless you can mentally put yourself in his shoes.

Yet too much recursion and too little discussion inevitably lead to wrong assumptions. Rather than explain their rationale, collaborators routinely assume the other person knows the reasons. Rather than compliment the other person on a good job, partners assume their praise would be redundant. Rather than ask for more information and listen closely, people assume they already know what the other person would say.

Assuming without verifying is dangerous. We are not mind readers; we are mind guessers. Sometimes we guess wrong. This is the reason why in partnerships that involve a risk of death — such as piloting an airplane, rock climbing, and scuba diving — the most important messages are mandated and standardized to remove any ambiguity.

At the Play It Again Sports store in Sydney, Nova Scotia, Canada, the managers and staff would commonly refer to each other as "kemosabe," a term introduced by the American radio and TV series *The Lone Ranger*. Part-owner Trevor Muller and his father, who sometimes helped out in the store, called each other "kemosabe" throughout their lives. It came to be a friendly greeting in the store between any two people, whether they were managers, employees, or customers.

But one store employee, Dorothy Kateri Moore, a member of the Mi'kmaq tribe, took offense, and after quitting her job, complained to the Nova Scotia Human Rights Commission. Her complaint led to a lengthy inquiry into why she was offended, what the Mullers meant by using the word "kemosabe," and even into how the fictional Lone Ranger and his Native American partner, Tonto, talked to each other.

"Kemosabe" was a term Tonto first called his partner. Where the scriptwriters got the word is unclear, and its precise meaning varies somewhat in the series. In the pilot episode of the TV series, Tonto says it means "trusty scout." In another episode, Tonto says it means "trusty friend." Although Tonto most often uses the term, sometimes the Lone Ranger uses it in return. "At no time during the episodes reviewed by this inquiry was the term 'kemosabe' ever used in a demeaning or derogatory manner or in any way that might be construed as a racial slur," stated the ruling.

"Tonto is the Lone Ranger's partner and friend," the judge determined. "He is clean cut, well groomed and although he speaks a form of broken English, he is neither dumb nor stupid. To the contrary, his role is to uncover many of the clues upon which the Lone Ranger's strategy is developed." The two men treat each other with respect, and while Native Americans, including Tonto, are often treated in a demeaning manner, the Lone Ranger never treats his counterpart poorly, the review determined. Moore's lawsuit was dismissed, and the decision was upheld by the Nova Scotia Court of Appeal.

As much as the case vindicated the store owner and gave judicial approval to the TV partnership, it also demonstrated the hazards of recursive thinking. The Mullers wrongly assumed that Moore would not be offended by a term that had been bandied about the store for some time. Moore wrongly assumed that the owner and his father were belittling her race.

And the cause of all the trouble was a single word.

THE PARTNERSHIP between Francis Crick and James D. Watson at Cambridge was built on communicating. Beyond that and their brilliance, they had little else.

In their quest to discover the molecular structure of DNA, Watson and Crick did not have a particularly pure sample of the genetic material like that possessed by Crick's friend Maurice Wilkins at rival King's College. They did not have the superior X-ray equipment controlled by Rosalind Franklin, another scientist at King's. They didn't have the head start of American biochemist Linus Pauling. At various points, they didn't really have permission to be working on the problem.

But both had expertise the other lacked, and they soon shared an obsession with decoding DNA. Most important, their regular communications, a source of great fulfillment for both partners, allowed them to combine their thinking and reach the discovery first.

Watson was a prodigy. He began attending the University of Chicago at age 15, receiving a degree in zoology four years later. He received his doctorate shortly after turning 22. "He was tall, stick-thin, socially ill at ease, and apt to snort with laughter halfway through a sentence," wrote one biographer. "He was also in the habit of speaking his mind with startling frankness."

Francis Crick was an English physicist whose interests veered toward biology. At an early age Crick shunned religion for science, which he found more insightful. His doctoral studies in physics stopped when a land mine destroyed his research on the viscosity of water at high pressure and temperature, what he later called "the dullest problem imaginable." From his experience with physics he had acquired "the hubris of the physicist, the feeling that physics as a discipline was highly successful, so why should not the other sciences do likewise?" He found the certainty of physics to be an antidote to what he perceived as "the rather plodding, somewhat cautious attitude" of biologists.

Watson and Crick met in October 1951, when Watson joined the Cavendish Laboratory at the University of Cambridge, where Crick was already working. They clicked immediately. Within half an hour, they were discussing the possibility of finding the structure of DNA. "From my first day in the lab I knew I would not leave Cambridge for a long time," wrote Watson. "Departing would be idiocy, for I had immediately discovered the fun of talking to Francis Crick."

Within a few days, they had a plan: They would use metal models, similar to children's construction sets, to think through the problem. Students today sometimes make models in school of the double helix of DNA using toothpicks and gumdrops, but the structure of the genetic material was very much a mystery in 1951.

To solve the puzzle required a tremendous amount of conjecture. The ability to bounce ideas off each other proved to be the principal strength of the collaboration between Crick and Watson. The American admired that Crick "never stops talking and thinking." The two men ate lunch together almost every day. Afterward, they would exchange ideas while strolling along the grounds. They shared coffee in the mornings and tea in the afternoons. When the group in Cavendish was offered an extra room, two of Watson and Crick's colleagues announced they were going to give it to them "so that you can talk to each other without disturbing the rest of us."

The bluntness of their exchanges made them productive. "By collaborating, if one of us got on the wrong track, one of us could get us out of it," Crick reminisced to Watson in a 1973 conversation. If one of them was convinced of a particular theory, the other would play devil's advocate to ensure they reached the right conclusion. "The other thing good about our collaboration was that we weren't the least bit afraid of being candid to each other, to the point of being rude," said Crick. "If you have constant interchange and chatting together and saying what you think of the other person's ideas to their face, I know that you can solve problems of this kind." The combination, as one colleague put it, was "that marvelous resonance between two minds — that high state in which 1 plus 1 does not equal 2 but more like 10."

At about the same time Watson and Crick were hitting it off, the pair that might have beaten them to the finish line got off on the wrong foot, never to recover. Rosalind Franklin, an expert in X-ray techniques, joined King's College in January 1951. She and Maurice Wilkins, already at King's, could well have discovered the structure of DNA had they communicated better.

"There isn't a first-class or even a good brain among them — in fact nobody with whom I particularly want to discuss anything, scientific or otherwise," Franklin wrote to a friend in Paris. At one point, she ordered Wilkins to stop his work on DNA. "Go back to your microscopes," she told him. At another, when Wilkins offered an insight, she ripped into him: "How dare you interpret my data for me!" Although Wilkins made overtures to Franklin, such as giving her a box of chocolates, she refused to work with him during the two crucial years when the discovery was within their reach. The acrimony became so bad that the head of the lab had to divide the instruments and DNA samples between them so they could work separately.

Crick and Watson made numerous mistakes along the way, giving little hint their exchanges would lead to a breakthrough. A visiting biochemist from Columbia University considered Watson "undeveloped," while Crick produced only "occasional nuggets glittering in the turbid stream of prattle." It was, he concluded, "a typical British intellectual atmosphere, little work and lots of talk."

Franklin eventually announced she was leaving King's College. Shortly before she left, Watson traveled to King's to visit Wilkins. Finding Wilkins busy, he walked down the hall to Franklin's lab. The door was ajar, and he walked in, finding her bent over an X-ray photo she was measuring. "Momentarily startled by my entry, she quickly regained her composure and, looking straight at my face, let her eyes tell me that uninvited guests should have the courtesy to knock," Watson recalled. As he began discussing his theories about DNA with Franklin, she became increasingly annoyed until the discussion turned into an argument.

"Rosy by then was hardly able to control her temper, and her voice rose as she told me that the stupidity of my remarks would be obvious if I would stop blubbering and look at her X-ray evidence," wrote Watson. Implying Franklin didn't know how to read the photos she was taking, he told her she needed to learn the theory of molecular structure to understand why her work did not disprove Watson's position. "Suddenly Rosy came from behind the lab bench that separated us and began moving toward me," wrote Watson. "Fearing that in her hot anger she might strike me, I . . . hastily retreated to the open door" just as Wilkins was poking his head into the room.

The two men went to have tea. Wilkins opened up as he had never before. "Now that I need no longer merely imagine the emotional hell he had faced during the past two years, he could treat me almost as a fellow collaborator rather than as a distant acquaintance with whom close confidences inevitably led to painful misunderstandings," wrote Watson.

They began to discuss DNA. Wilkins mentioned that Franklin's photos, which had been turned over to him in preparation for her leaving, showed a particular pattern for the structure of DNA. Watson asked what the pattern looked like. Wilkins went in the next room and retrieved one of the clearest photos.

"The instant I saw the picture my mouth fell open and my pulse began to race," wrote Watson. Thoughts clicked that, in hindsight, Crick and Watson could have seen earlier, but didn't.

With new information and new urgency, Crick and Watson returned to their model building. First Crick worked through a problem that defied Watson. While Watson was playing tennis one afternoon, Crick rebuilt the model to the new specifications so the double helix had the right amount of twist. He attached a note for his collaborator: "This is it — 36 degrees rotation."

Picking up where Crick left off, Watson cut cardboard pieces to represent the molecules in the middle of the double helix. Suddenly, as he tried to fit the pieces to each other, he noticed something crucial: When two of the four kinds of molecules were matched, they made the same shape as when the remaining two kinds of molecules were combined. DNA looks a little like a spiral staircase. Watson had just discovered how equal-sized stairs were made throughout the helix. By putting their heads together and playing with puzzle pieces, Crick and Watson had discovered the key to how the pattern of life is passed from one generation to the next.

Neither man was eager to tell Wilkins. Just as the two partners finished adjusting the angles and distances in their model of DNA, a letter arrived from Wilkins, welcoming collaboration. "I think you will be interested to know that our dark lady leaves us next week," Wilkins wrote to Crick. "I am now reasonably clear of other commitments and have started up a general offensive on Nature's secret strongholds. . . . At last the decks are clear and we can put all hands to the pumps! It won't be long now." Crick was looking at the model as he read his friend's letter.

Much has been made of Wilkins showing Franklin's X-ray photo to Watson. Some say she was robbed of her achievement. Others point out that she built on Wilkins' work and had turned it back over to him. Some say it was an improper breach. Others argue that the photo had already been revealed in public meetings. Rarely discussed, however, is how Franklin's refusal to collaborate, freshly punctuated by her angry exchange with Watson, almost certainly cost her the respect, professional courtesy, and credit many commentators say she deserved. Through her irascibility and go-it-alone attitude, Franklin's wound was largely self-inflicted, and she became less a scientific pioneer than a cautionary tale.

In 1953, Watson and Crick submitted their breakthrough to the British journal *Nature*. In one of the greatest understatements ever published, the men began their paper: "We wish to suggest a structure for the salt of deoxyribose nucleic acid (D.N.A.). This structure has novel features which are of considerable biological interest." To determine whose name would appear first on the paper, they flipped a coin. The two men invited Wilkins to add his name to the paper, but he declined.

In 1962, all three men shared the Nobel Prize for medicine for their DNA work. Franklin was not considered, as she died in 1958, and Nobel rules forbid posthumous awards. Substantial conjecture surrounds the question of whether she would have been honored had she been alive.

The larger question revolves around what she and Wilkins might have accomplished if they had worked together. "It was a pity that Rosalind and I did not spend more time discussing the importance of her discovery and what it might tell us about the structure of DNA," Wilkins wrote in his autobiography. He questioned what he might have done differently. Perhaps he should have asserted himself more, he speculated. "It may seem amazing that at the time neither of us saw the obvious explanation," wrote Wilkins. "If she and I had discussed the problem there would have been little to prevent us finding the Double Helix."

Chapter Eight

Unselfishness

✯✯

"I've always hated the danger part of climbing, and it's great to come down again because it's safe. But there is something about building up a comradeship — that I still believe is the greatest of all feats — and sharing in the dangers with your company of peers. It's the intense effort, the giving of everything you've got. It's really a very pleasant sensation."

— Sir Edmund Hillary

ERNEST SHACKLETON, FRANK WILD, and their two fellow explorers were starving. Three weeks earlier, they reached closer to the South Pole than men had ever traveled before. They turned back in a desperate race against starvation and the scheduled departure of a ship waiting for them on the edge of the Antarctic continent.

They were working their way between food depots set up for their return journey. Several times, they ran out of food before finding the next depot. At one point, the team had only enough biscuits to ration one in the morning to each man.

Wild was ill and extremely weak, unable to eat the dried meat and lard mixture that was the staple of the expedition. He devoured his single biscuit. As they set out to find the next cache of food, Shackleton took his biscuit and put it in Wild's pocket.

"What's that, Boss?" asked Wild.

"Your need is greater than mine," said the leader.

Wild was so awe-struck that he underlined every word of the story when he recounted it in his journal: "S[hackleton] privately forced upon me his one breakfast biscuit, and would have given me another tonight had I allowed him. I do not suppose that anyone else in the world can thoroughly realize how much generosity and sympathy was shown by this; I do, and by God I shall never forget. Thousands of pounds would not have bought that one biscuit."

With the nourishment of the biscuit, Wild was able to go on, and through the fortunate discovery of each of the food stores along the way, to regain his strength. He vowed never to return to Antarctica.

His resolve did not last long. "On the return journey, while sharing a tent with Shackleton, he asked me if I would join him on another attempt at the Pole," wrote Wild. "One of my diary entries reads like this: 'This trip has completely cured me of any desire for further polar exploration. Nothing will ever tempt me to face that awful glacier and terrible plateau again.' However, so great was my regard for the 'Boss' that without any hesitation I replied, 'Yes!' We then went on to discuss details."

Five years later, Shackleton led the voyage of the *Endurance*, a ship that was crushed in ice, forcing the men on a heroic journey to an uninhabited island and an improbable rescue of every crew member. The journey made Shackleton famous, and it led to generations studying his leadership abilities.

Because of the trust built during the earlier expedition, Wild was Shackleton's second in command on the *Endurance*; he was the one Shackleton entrusted with the care of most of the men as the leader and five others went for help in a small boat. "Wild never forgot the private act of kindness" with the biscuit, wrote author Caroline Alexander, "and his adamantine loyalty to Shackleton would prove to be one of the expedition's major assets."

THE SACRIFICES SOME PARTNERS MAKE for each other don't make sense. A partnership is based on the assumption that by working together, both people will achieve heights neither could have accomplished alone. You and your collaborator are supposed to be better off than you would be without the working relationship. While looking out for the other person creates trust, endangering your life for him seems to miss the point. What good is a partnership to a person who gets himself killed for someone else?

Since Charles Darwin published *On the Origin of the Species* in 1859, the scientific yardstick by which all behaviors have been judged is their effect on the survival of a creature or its family. Habits, instincts, or biases that reduce the risk of death, increase the odds of reproducing, or serve to protect a person's children are behaviors that are more likely to continue and spread through succeeding generations. From an evolutionary perspective, looking out too much for the other guy, unless it helps you or your family, is counterproductive. True altruism is not sustainable, according to these theories, because it doesn't get passed on as well as more selfish tactics.

This doesn't mean it never makes sense to collaborate. Darwin himself postulated that teamwork was a superior biological trait. "When two tribes of primeval man, living in the same country, came into competition, if (other circumstances being equal) the one tribe included a great number of courageous, sympathetic and faithful members, who were always ready to warn each other of danger, to aid and defend each other, this tribe would succeed better and conquer the other," he wrote. "The advantage which disciplined soldiers have over undisciplined hordes follows chiefly from the confidence which each man feels in his comrades.... Selfish and contentious people will not cohere, and without coherence nothing can be effected. A tribe rich in the above qualities would spread and be victorious over other tribes."

Using Darwin's rationale, scientists are not impressed by most partnerships. They usually find some way to explain that what appears to be unselfishness on the surface pays off for the one who did the good deed. "Instrumental reciprocity," they call it — a means to a self-serving end: If I can keep my partner happy, he'll do what I need him to do for me. It's nothing more than a deal, a mutually beneficial arrangement.

Some believe human nature works against every behavior that cannot ultimately be traced to a genetically selfish reason. "Be warned," wrote Richard Dawkins in his book *The Selfish Gene*, "that if you wish, as I do, to build a society in which individuals cooperate generously and unselfishly towards a common good, you can expect little help from biological nature."

Instrumental reciprocity is common and can be quite constructive. Much of this book describes how the right partnerships, properly managed, create the optimal strategy for your success. All partnerships begin as instrumental agreements. In the early stages, they could even be called mutually selfish. For many collaborations, this coming together so that both partners go away richer is enough to carry the partnership all the way to the goal.

But then there's that biscuit.

Why would Shackleton endanger himself to feed his partner? Why would Wild sign on for another expedition on which he nearly died? Why do soldiers sometimes sacrifice their lives for their unrelated comrades? Why do the selfish gene's greatest defenders revolt at its Hobbesian cruelty? "My own feeling," wrote Dawkins, "is that a human society based simply on the gene's law of universal ruthless selfishness would be a very nasty society in which to live." It is difficult to write off selfless acts as simply the irrational tactics of people who don't understand how the game should be played.

Three statements about unselfishness from Gallup's research proved to be the ultimate measures of the strength of a partnership:

- We take as much satisfaction at seeing the other succeed as we do from our own success.

- My partner will risk a lot for me, and I will do the same for him or her.

- My partner is like a brother or a sister to me.

Good working relationships average at least 3.3 on these statements on a 1-to-5 scale. Those in excellent partnerships strongly agree with all three statements. As extreme as the final statement is, the question of whether you have formed a fraternal bond with your counterpart discriminates between successful and poor alliances better than any of the other statements Gallup tested. It raises fascinating questions about how humans blur the genetic boundaries for those they have come to know well and regard highly in a major endeavor.

None of the traditional economic models, evolutionary extrapolations, or game strategies explains why humans' highest ideals are fundamentally unselfish — the Golden Rule, the Good Samaritan, and the admonition that

"Greater love hath no man than this, that a man lay down his life for his friends."

They don't explain why Benjamin Franklin took pleasure in lending money with a pay-it-forward condition that ensured he would never see the cash again. "I do not pretend to give such a sum; I only lend it to you," he wrote in the letter that accompanied the money. "When you meet with another honest man in similar distress, you must pay me by lending this sum to him; enjoining him to discharge the debt by a like operation, when he shall be able, and shall meet with another opportunity. I hope it may thus go through many hands, before it meets with a knave that will stop its progress."

There are hints in various studies that something deeper, something more meaningful, is going on in the minds of great collaborators. Some studies show that the act of cooperating itself, apart from the tangible benefits it brings, is intrinsically rewarding. The brain's reactions "extend beyond players' processing of outcomes, such as monetary gain, usually associated with mutual cooperation in human societies, and reflect emotional responses based on social and moral judgments."

There are intriguing clues about why humans enjoy making others happy, such as how various hot spots in the brain coordinate to impose moral values on ordinary social events. A part of the brain that tracks the actions of others may be partly responsible for a reflex remarkably similar to the Golden Rule. "Perhaps altruism did not grow out of a warm-glow feeling of doing good for others, but out of the simple recognition that that thing over there is a person that has intentions and goals. And therefore, I might want to treat them like I might want them to treat me," said study author Scott Huettel, an associate professor of psychology at Duke University Medical Center.

If we valued most those strategies that best fit the selfish gene, our highest ideal would be Tit for Tat, not the Good Samaritan. Yet we aim for something higher. "Self-sacrifice does not follow the rules of evolutionary biology," wrote collaborators Ernst Fehr and Suzann-Viola Renninger. "If the immediate family does not profit and if [there is no] future advantage, then selflessness gains nothing. Worse, it is costly in terms of resources, health, or money. By this logic, there really should not be any Good Samaritans. Yet they clearly exist."

Feelings of moral obligation come naturally to people. For a species allegedly controlled by selfish genes, we have an incredible capacity and reverence for unselfishness. Many people can't resist finding religious overtones in our noblest motivations. "In an age of enlightenment and secularization, scientists such as Charles Darwin shocked contemporaries when they questioned the special status of human beings and attempted to classify them on a continuum with all other species. Humans were stripped of all that was godlike," wrote Fehr and Renninger. "Today biology is restoring to them something of that former exalted position. Our species is apparently the only one with a genetic makeup that promotes selflessness and true altruistic behavior."

While most working relationships start as calculated alliances, a remarkably large proportion of good partnerships advance to a higher plane. This level goes by different names. Sometimes it's called "mutuality." Academicians occasionally use the clumsy phrase "self-other merging." In the vernacular, it's sometimes called "kinship." Liv Arnesen used the Norwegian word *søstersjel*, a "sister soul." This bond occurs when each partner ceases looking at the arrangement strictly in terms of what it does for him and begins genuinely concerning himself with the happiness of his counterpart.

Unselfishness changes everything about collaboration. When you value your partner's rewards as much as you do your own, concerns over fairness either melt away or go in the opposite direction. "What's in it for me?" becomes "What is my counterpart getting out of this?" "Am I being paid enough?" becomes "Am I being paid too much compared with my partner?" Waiting for the next perfect message from a counterpart becomes a concern with finding the most considerate way to communicate with him or her. "Is my partner doing enough?" becomes "Am I doing enough?" If a person values his comrade getting a reward as much as he does getting one himself, the optimal solution is always collaborative.

Science does not now and may never have all the answers as to why many partnerships, despite the compelling reasons to the contrary, reach the level of true unselfishness. But something about us deeply appreciates that they do.

✷✷

Daniel Kahneman was an early student of psychology. The gossip he heard around his family's home in Paris intrigued him. "I grew up in a world that consisted exclusively of people and words, and most of the words were about people," he wrote. He found people to be complex and interesting. "Some people were better than others, but the best were far from perfect and no one was simply bad. Most of [the] stories were touched by irony, and they all had two sides or more," he explained.

He was just a boy when Nazi troops overran France. As a Jew, he was expected to wear the Star of David on his clothes and to be home by 6 p.m. Going out to play with a Christian friend one day, he stayed beyond the curfew and turned his sweater inside out to hide the emblem while he walked the several blocks back home.

"As I was walking down an empty street, I saw a German soldier approaching," he recalled. "He was wearing the black uniform that I had been told to fear more than others — the one worn by specially recruited SS soldiers. As I came closer to him, trying to walk fast, I noticed that he was looking at me intently. Then he beckoned me over, picked me up, and hugged me. I was terrified that he would notice the star inside my sweater. He was speaking to me with great emotion, in German. When he put me down, he opened his wallet, showed me a picture of a boy, and gave me some money. I went home more certain than ever that my mother was right: People were endlessly complicated and interesting."

After the war, Kahneman and his family immigrated to Palestine. The young man remained interested in how people think. He was more interested in what made people believe in God than in whether that belief is justified, more curious about why people find something right or wrong than in the ethics themselves. His interests deepened as he was exposed to neuropsychology at Hebrew University in Jerusalem and later, when he was drafted into the Israel Defense Forces, assigned to its psychology branch. He gravitated toward the difficulty of trying to predict human behavior.

One of the puzzles Kahneman happened across was a lieutenant in the ranks of the paratroopers. The officer was pale; he had been wounded. During a live-fire exercise, the lieutenant had ordered a non-commissioned officer to place a long metal tube loaded with explosives under the barbed wire of a position the unit was attacking. The explosion was supposed to blow open a gap where the troops could break through. The soldier placed the charge, lit the fuse, and then froze in place. Realizing that the soldier was just seconds from being killed, the lieutenant leapt from the rock he was using for cover and knocked the soldier out of harm's way before the detonation. The lieutenant was wounded in the act of saving his comrade.

In 1969, Kahneman teamed up with a younger associate in Jerusalem to work on a joint paper. They were writing about several quirks of human nature, such as the tendency for people to believe that a coin flipped heads will be more likely to balance things out by coming up tails in subsequent tosses. It turned out that Kahneman's new colleague was the same lieutenant who risked his life to save one of his soldiers. His name was Amos Tversky.

Kahneman discovered that his new collaborator had talents he lacked. Tversky's style was confident and crisp, and it made Kahneman's ideas come across stronger on the page. He was a skilled writer with "an uncanny sense of direction," Kahneman recalled. "With him, movement was always forward. Progress might be slow, but each of the myriad of successive drafts that we produced was an improvement — this was not something I could take for granted when working on my own. . . . I was conscious of how much better it was than the more hesitant piece I would have written by myself."

"The experience was magical," Kahneman recalled. "I had enjoyed collaborative work before, but this was something different." It wasn't just Tversky's intelligence — people sometimes said he was the smartest person they knew — but he was also funny, with a joke for every situation. "In his presence, I became funny as well, and the result was that we could spend hours of solid work in continuous mirth," wrote Kahneman. When they finished their first joint paper, the men flipped a coin to decide whose name would come first on the publication.

In working with Tversky, Kahneman found the perfect work partner, someone with whom he would collaborate closely for the next decade. The two men found that their minds clicked in amazing ways. "Some of the greatest joys of our collaboration — and probably much of its success — came from our ability to elaborate each other's nascent thoughts," wrote Kahneman. "If I expressed a half-formed idea, I knew that Amos would be there to understand it, probably more clearly than I did, and that if it had merit he would see it. Like most people, I am somewhat cautious about exposing tentative thoughts to others — I must first make sure that they [the thoughts] are not idiotic. In the best years of the collaboration, this caution was completely absent. The mutual trust and the complete lack of defensiveness that we achieved were particularly remarkable because both of us — Amos even more than I — were known to be severe critics. . . . Amos and I shared the wonder of together owning a goose that could lay golden eggs — a joint mind that was better than our separate minds."

Because Kahneman was a morning person and Tversky was a night owl, they fell into a pattern of meeting for lunch and spending long afternoons working together. They talked a lot, not just about the research, but about everything. Both learned how the other thought, and each could sometimes complete his counterpart's sentences. There was no explicit division of labor; they wrote their questionnaires and papers together.

When they disagreed, they discussed the issue until it was resolved. They agreed that if they were stuck on whether a certain reference should be included in a paper, Tversky would make the final call. If they disagreed how to resolve a grammatical issue, Kahneman would decide. After the original coin toss put Tversky's name first, they alternated the order of names on subsequent papers. In time, their colleagues began calling them the "dynamic duo."

Their research and writing became some of the most important work in the field now known as behavioral economics. Traditional economics examines social problems from the perspective of a hypothetical, highly rational person — a person who, it turns out, doesn't exist. It uses a tremendous amount of math, much of it calculations the average person cannot follow, to determine how various incentives should influence people's actions. Behavioral economics focuses on how real-life human reactions differ from the prediction of what a purely rational being would do. Like the selfish gene theory, traditional economics predicts much less cooperation between people than is found when behavioral economists actually put people together and watch them cooperate. One is based on theory, the other on reality.

People don't think like computers, Tversky and Kahneman argued. They reach decisions through rules of thumb subject to mortal biases that lead to severe and systematic errors. People "systematically violate the axioms of expected utility theory," they wrote in one paper. The theory of decision making, they wrote in a subsequent paper, "was conceived as a normative model of an idealized decision maker, not as a description of the behavior of real people."

Through numerous insights into the way real people make real decisions, Kahneman and Tversky became luminaries in behavioral economics. They did so despite the fact, or maybe because of the fact, that they were not economists but psychologists. Tversky once described his work as taking a scientific view of patterns that were well-known to advertisers and used-car salesmen. A large proportion of the academic studies conducted on the partner's dilemma, on the brains of people interacting with someone else, on the issue of fairness between collaborators, and on how reputations are formed make at least one reference to Tversky and Kahneman.

In 1978, Kahneman and his wife moved to British Columbia, Canada, while Tversky and his wife settled in Stanford, California. "Amos and I were then at the peak of our joint game, and completely committed to our collaboration. For a few years, we managed to maintain it, by spending every second weekend together and by placing multiple phone calls each day, some lasting several hours," Kahneman recalled. "But eventually the goose that had laid the golden eggs languished, and our collaboration tapered off. Although this outcome now appears inevitable, it came as a painful surprise to us. We had completely failed to appreciate how critically our successful interaction had depended on our being together at the birth of every significant idea, on our rejection of any formal division of labor, and on the infinite patience that became a luxury when we could meet only periodically. We struggled for years to revive the magic we had lost, but in vain."

Even as Kahneman moved to other universities — Berkeley and then Princeton — the two men stayed in touch and collaborated as best they could from a distance. Well-thought-of before they began collaborating, the men were even more highly respected because of their work together, and each went on to other fruitful partnerships and additional regard in the scientific community.

Then circumstances conspired to end Kahneman and Tversky's collaboration before either man was done. In early 1996, Tversky was diagnosed with skin cancer that had metastasized. He had only a few months to live. With so little time, he and his longtime collaborator determined to take on one last project, to edit a book on decision making that would describe work in the field since the two men began their partnership.

"We planned an ambitious preface as a joint project, but I think we both knew from the beginning that we would not be granted enough time to complete it," wrote Kahneman. In June of 1996, Tversky died. "The preface I wrote alone," recalled the surviving partner, "was probably my most painful writing experience."

In 2002, Daniel Kahneman was awarded the Nobel Prize in economics. It is widely speculated that Amos Tversky would have shared the award had he lived long enough. Unable to claim the honor with his collaborator,

Kahneman brought along his friend's memory in the form of a large photo of Tversky he projected on the screen at the beginning of the prize lecture. "The work on which the award was given was done jointly with Amos Tversky during a long period of unusually close collaboration," Kahneman told the audience. "He should have been here."

In his Nobel Prize autobiography, Kahneman went into detail about the rewards of collaborating with Tversky, his great admiration for him, and his tremendous feeling of personal loss at his absence. "There is less intelligence in the world," he wrote. "There is less wit. There are many questions that will never be answered with the same inimitable combination of depth and clarity. There are standards that will not be defended with the same mix of principle and good sense. Life has become poorer. There is a large Amos-shaped gap in the mosaic, and it will not be filled."

"The 12 or 13 years in which most of our work was joint were years of interpersonal and intellectual bliss," wrote the Nobel laureate. "Everything was interesting, almost everything was funny, and there was the recurrent joy of seeing an idea take shape."

Kahneman ended his life story with a compliment to his fellow researcher: "I have almost never had that experience with anyone else. If you have not had it, you don't know how marvelous collaboration can be."

In Closing

Looking Within

BEING A GREAT PARTNER IS HARD WORK.

If you are striving for a goal by yourself, the entire endeavor can be subject to your whims. Want to change the objective? Go ahead. Want to go faster or slower? No one will object. Something doesn't go as planned? You have no one to blame but yourself.

Add another person to the equation, and the potential for problems explodes. The two of you must always stay on the common ground of a shared mission. Both of you are apt to overestimate your own contributions, to see the other's weaknesses clearer than his strengths, to find the other's way of doing things odd, to make wrong assumptions and communicate too little, and perhaps to find trust itself elusive. The most dangerous trap of collaboration is the convenient availability of someone else to blame for its failure.

Those who have experienced a great collaboration say there are many reasons not to enter into one. "It's harder than it looks and more trouble than it's worth," one successful partner joked.

Collaborating well demands a degree of accommodation and humility rarely needed otherwise. It can require exceptional diplomatic abilities, awareness, countering your natural biases, and the flexibility to incorporate another strong ego into the demands of your own. Occasionally, it requires great self-control and forgiveness. In all cases, it demands an intense desire to achieve the mutual goal that overcomes what Tenzing Norgay called the "small bickerings and resentments," the "molehills" that interfere with scaling the mountain.

If you want to have great partnerships, be a great partner. Get beyond yourself. Give up the notion that you are well-rounded, and stop expecting your colleagues to be universally proficient. Incorporate someone else's motivations into your view of the accomplishment. Loosen up. Put aside your competitive nature, your prepackaged view of how the thing should be done, and your desire not to be inconvenienced with the imperfections of a fellow human being. Focus more on what you do for the partnership than what you get from it. Demonstrate trust in more people, and see if they don't surprise you with their trustworthiness. Be slower to anger and quicker to forgive. And along the way, communicate continuously.

As you do, incredible things will happen. You will discover more comrades among your colleagues. You will find greater strengths in yourself and in your collaborators.

Your happiness will increase. You will achieve greater heights than you thought attainable. Most important, you will not stand alone on these summits.

That is the Power of 2.

Additional Insights for Businesspeople

For Managers: A Boss or a Partner?

For Leaders: Creating Collaborative Organizations

A Boss or a Partner?

"A manager is an assistant to his men."
— IBM founder Thomas J. Watson

MOST OF THE SCHOLARLY WORK ON PARTNERSHIPS assumes the two players have equal power. The partner's dilemma usually pairs up two players who receive identical rewards for cooperating or unilaterally defecting, the same punishments for being suckered or for mutual betrayal. These lab settings match real-life situations when a manager gives two employees a shared task, an instructor assigns two students a joint paper, or two volunteers agree to team up for a good cause.

Yet many of the most important collaborative opportunities arise when one person in a pair has power over the other. It's not unusual for one of the partners to have the ear of the CEO, to be a member of the family that owns the company, to control the purse strings, or some other coercive capacity not matched by the other person. In many potential partnerships, one person is the manager of the other. These can be some of the most frustrating relationships, particularly for the less powerful partner.

An employee's collaborative relationship with his supervisor is more than twice as likely to show up in the negative column than in the positive one, according to Gallup's research. When asked to name someone with whom they have had a poor partnership, 32 percent of people name their manager. When asked to name someone with whom they've had a good partnership, only 15 percent name their manager.

The most fundamental misunderstanding about partnerships between managers and the managed is that they should not exist at all. Sixteen percent of managers flat-out admit they are more like a boss than a partner to those they supervise. According to this line of thinking, partnerships exist only between equals. "I'm not the manager because I'm always right, but I'm always right because I'm the manager," said major league baseball manager Gene Mauch, the most frequently winning manager to have never won a pennant and architect of some of the game's longest losing streaks.

Eighty-four percent of managers claim they are more a partner than a boss, but many of those who report to them would beg to differ. Among employees, only 53 percent say their manager is more like a partner than a boss.

The same attributes that make a good partnership between equals make a good alliance between managers and employees: complementary strengths, a common mission, fairness, trust, acceptance, forgiveness, communicating, and unselfishness.

Although most employees understand running the business requires some people to give direction and others to take it, they still value being treated as an equal by their manager. It's a high standard to live up to, but it pays great dividends.

Differences in rank can be deceiving, creating the impression that the "subordinate" has few alternatives should her "superior" flex his muscles and enforce compliance. The evidence indicates just the opposite. Employees may lack official authority, but their informal power is substantial. Executives, managers, and other higher ranking partners do better when they build a partnership than when they exercise command.

When research partners Ernst Fehr and Simon Gächter wanted to understand the dilemmas faced by employers and employees, they created a small-scale job market and watched it in action. Their volunteers were randomly assigned to be either someone buying work (employers) or selling it (employees). The buyers announced what level of work quality they wanted and what they were willing to pay for it. Then the sellers got the chance to decide individually whether to take a job, which to choose, and what level of work they would give. Only one employee at a time could work for each employer. To give more power to the employers, six buyers were matched with eight sellers, guaranteeing the prospect of "unemployment."

Fehr and Gächter devised two sets of rules for their laboratory labor market. In the first, the employee could "shirk," giving lower quality work than the employer bid for, without any penalty to the worker. The researchers called this the "trust" condition. In the second condition, the manager had a one-in-three chance of verifying whether his worker shirked, and if he had, the boss could impose a fine. This was called the "incentive" condition.

Long-standing economic theories predict that the employees should work harder under threat of having their pay docked. The incentive scenario is supposed to provide a way for the employer to offer higher wages for better work because he can enforce those expectations. When the employer cannot punish slacking, so the logic goes, the employee has every selfish reason to give low-quality work, and knowing this, the employer has every reason to make only a minimum wage offer.

This conventional wisdom is wrong. The employees who were trusted and not coerced agreed to work harder than those whose compliance was forced. "Voluntary cooperation may indeed be undermined by incentive contracts," wrote Fehr and Gächter. When employers have the option, they usually choose more fines and less pay. This backfires, causing low work levels that ensure the employer pays the price for his penny pinching. "Even if the buyers combine the threat of fining with the payment of relatively high prices, the sellers' voluntary cooperation remains low," they concluded. It is a sense of moral obligation, not the point of an economic spear, that motivates the best levels of performance.

In manager-employee relationships as in peer-to-peer collaborations, reciprocity is more powerful than rationality. The difference in rank is not enough to change the friend-or-foe wiring and the extreme positive and negative reactions on both sides of the switch. With their managers as much as with their peers, people mirror what they perceive coming from the other person. To what's given begrudgingly, they return begrudgingly. To what's given generously, they reciprocate generously.

Nowhere has this been demonstrated more exhaustively than in Gallup's international employee engagement database. At this printing, the repository holds the responses from 15 million surveys of managers and employees, gathered in 63 languages and in 163 countries. These respondents rated their level of agreement with 12 crucial statements about their work environment, many of which focus on the tenor of their relationship with their manager. "My supervisor, or someone at work, seems to care about me as a person," states one of the items. Other items focus on aspects such as the employee feeling connected to the mission of the company, having the chance to use her strengths every day, getting recognition for good work, feeling as though her opinions count, and having someone talk to her about her progress.

Workgroups headed by a "partner" have nearly twice the proportion of engaged employees compared to those led by a "boss." Engaged employees deliver higher levels of performance to their managers and organizations without the need for coercion. When business units in the most engaged quartile of the Gallup global database are compared with those in the least engaged quartile, the more engaged workgroups show 27 percent less absenteeism, 31 to 51 percent lower turnover, 62 percent fewer accidents, 12 percent better customer scores, 18 percent higher productivity, and 12 percent higher profitability.

When combined, these studies make it clear there is simply no way a manager who's boss can get the same results from a team that a partner can.

For Leaders

Creating Collaborative Organizations

★★

"The problem is nearly intractable because of the way the government is currently structured. . . . It is hard to 'break down stovepipes' when there are so many stoves that are legally and politically entitled to have cast-iron pipes of their own."

— Final Report of the National Commission on the Terrorist Attacks Upon the United States

GUY GANNETT COMMUNICATIONS was a family-owned company in Maine determined to create a partnership that would revolutionize the media world. In the mid-1990s, the firm embarked on a strategy of increasing collaboration between its largest newspaper, the *Portland Press Herald*, and its Portland TV station, WGME. They were entering a new "dimension," the leaders proclaimed.

Under U.S. antitrust laws, a company cannot maintain a duopoly by owning a daily newspaper and a TV station in the same market. But the rule does not apply to businesses that owned both properties before the 1972 regulation went into effect.

Wanting to make the most of their legal exemption, Guy Gannett officials began encouraging "synergy" between the two previously autonomous units. Committees of executives from both properties were formed. The TV station and the newspaper commissioned shared market research. The respective advertising departments were pushed closer together, first gently, then explicitly. So were the print and broadcast news operations.

"We could not just rely on their good nature and good intentions," said James B. Shaffer, Guy Gannett's CEO at the time. "Only reorganizing the company broke loose collaborative sales." Various TV and newspaper leaders who disagreed with the strategy or doubted its longevity left or were dismissed. "New managers came in, and I went out," wrote former *Press Herald* Editor-in-Chief Lou Ureneck. "One day you're a hero; the next day you're meeting with an employment counselor at your former employer's expense and trying to rearrange your identity."

The strategy began to take hold. Some of the TV and newspaper salespeople began making joint calls to advertisers. The lead headlines from the next day's *Press Herald* were announced on WGME's 11 p.m. newscast, and the TV station's meteorologists and forecasts were featured on the newspaper's weather page. Such collaboration "better serves readers and viewers journalistically," said Bruce J. Gensmer, a company executive appointed to bring both media together. "The hearts and minds of advertisers won't be far behind."

But cynicism about the new partnership ran deep through the Old Port offices of the *Press Herald* and those of the CBS affiliate four miles on the other side of Back Cove. Any TV-side employee who jumped in with both feet risked being played for a fool by her newspaper-side counterpart, and vice versa. Some employees doubted the assertions of company Chairwoman Madeleine Corson, Guy Gannett's granddaughter, that the company was committed for the long haul to owning and integrating both media. Newspaper-TV synergy was the flavor of the month, they said.

Then, on April Fools' Day of 1998, the skeptics were proven right. Corson and her uncle and fellow company trustee, John H. Gannett, announced they were putting the business on the auction block. Game over. The sale would close the antitrust loophole, forcing the *Press Herald* and WGME to go to separate buyers and become competitors again. Partnerships that were required one day were forbidden the next.

After the newspaper was sold to one buyer and the TV station to another, the Gannett family was left more than half a billion dollars richer. Their former employees were left confused. Just as the government orator in George Orwell's *1984* announced that the old ally was the new enemy and the old enemy the new ally, the *Press Herald* announced a "news-sharing partnership" with a different TV station, Portland ABC affiliate WMTW, whose executive vice president made collaborative noises of his own: "What I'm trying to do here is build a multilevel news-delivery platform."

Those who took jobs with Gannett and moved their families to Maine to be part of the original collaboration and those incumbent employees who invested their best efforts to make the TV-newspaper partnership work got fooled.

The cruel paradox was that the same leaders of the company who, early in the process, could not understand why some people resisted the initiative later demonstrated why those cynics were dead on.

The "new dimension" Guy Gannett Communication's leaders said they were entering is, in fact, a very old one. Every organization faces issues of collaboration, getting various departments to cooperate with each other, trying to make the most of a marketing alliance with another company, or working through a merger or acquisition.

The more consequential *New York Times* and *USA Today* struggled to get their online and print divisions to work better together. "Over the past 10 years the newsroom of Nytimes.com and the (print) newsroom on 43rd Street have been partners at a distance — separated administratively, culturally, geographically and financially," *Times* Executive Editor Bill Keller wrote in a 2005 memo to his staff. "We have built bridges ... and we have admired each other's work, but we have not been full collaborators."

The commission created to investigate security breaches preceding the September 11, 2001, attacks on the United States found, among other issues, a serious lack of collaboration among the various U.S. intelligence agencies. Those agencies now answer to the new Office of the Director of National Intelligence (ODNI) under the charge that they find better ways of working together. "In the past, the Intelligence Community was siloed into discrete disciplines and functions. These silos often led to competition and duplication," states an unclassified ODNI strategy outline. "We must transcend the current agency-based linear model . . . and develop a more mission-based model that is fluid, synchronizes collection, collaborates on analytic issues in real time, and broadens our partnership strategy."

Leaders often say, "We need more partnerships" between — you name it — education and industry, public and private sectors, one campus in the university system and another. "We need more partnerships, more joint ventures, and more alliances" to solve the energy issues facing the world, said BP Group Chief Executive Tony Hayward. "The time has come to develop new forms of contractual relationships that move beyond the historical model."

Wells Fargo merged with Wachovia Corporation. Delta Airlines merged with Northwest Airlines. Sirius Satellite Radio acquired XM Satellite Radio. Exxon merged with Mobil. The list is long.

Mergers. Acquisitions. Joint marketing agreements. Strategic alliances. Collaborative ventures. Organizational integration. There are dozens of terms for the strategy of bringing together — sometimes forcing together — two entities on the assumption that when united they can accomplish what neither enterprise could do alone. But they all refer to the same problem: how to create a collaborative organization.

The track record of these combinations is poor. Executives overseeing an integration routinely tell Wall Street the new, bigger firm will give unrivalled service to its customers, new opportunities to its employees, and higher returns to its shareholders. They're usually wrong. More than half of these plans fail.

A study of nearly 5,000 mergers and acquisitions found that the target companies not only suffer the "natural and acceptable" loss of many executives shortly after the combination, but "leadership continuity is permanently altered once the firm is acquired. Target companies can expect to lose 21 percent or more of their executives each year — more than double that experienced in non-merged firms — for at least 10 years after the acquisition!"

More often than not, the two firms fail to integrate, fail to realize the promised synergy, lose momentum on key projects the companies were implementing before the merger, lose executives with years of experience and knowledge about the firms, and ignore "negative effects of the merger on target employees that eventually erode productivity."

"We may not perform as well financially as we expected following the merger," US Airways warned investors after its 2005 merger with America West. Once reality set in, the airline announced that the process of combining "will be costly, complex, and time-consuming," and management "will have to devote substantial efforts to such integration that could otherwise be spent on operational matters or other strategic opportunities."

Whether pushing together companies or departments, leaders usually fail to realize the complexities into which they are getting themselves. The combination of Group A and Group B looks clean only on paper. In practice, it is the messy business of hundreds or thousands of employees from Group A each working with 1, 2, or 10 people from Group B, and vice versa. Strangers come in. Trusted associates leave or are laid off. Thousands have new working relationships imposed on them at a time of intense uncertainty and vulnerability.

There is a reason parts of a company are called divisions. Most often, they are divided from the rest of the organization, pursuing their own ends, suspicious of those outside their fold. "To simply assume . . . that the transformation will succeed or the myriad issues and concerns associated with it will work themselves out in the long run is naïve," wrote one authority on the subject. "A merger or acquisition is ultimately a human process."

A collaborative organization is like a zipper. To work, both sides must be firmly fastened together from top to bottom. Individual partnerships between people from each entity are like the interlocking teeth of the zipper that hold it together. When teeth are separated or missing, it threatens the entire bond between the two sides.

One of the most common fatal flaws in creating a collaborative organization is failing to pursue a common mission, a goal premised on an agreement that both camps will succeed together.

As the Union Army made plans in late 1862 to take Vicksburg, Mississippi, President Abraham Lincoln gave General John McClernand secret orders to organize troops for an attempt at the city. But General Ulysses S. Grant was already pursuing the same goal, and no one made sure they were united in the endeavor.

"Vicksburg was 250 miles away, and as (Grant) saw it the town belonged to the man who got there first," wrote historian Shelby Foote. At one point when Grant would normally have waited for reinforcements, he instead proceeded south. "I feared that delay might bring McClernand," the general wrote later. The Union subsequently lost the Battle of Chickasaw Bayou, the first contest in what became a six-month campaign. Grant was "fighting two wars simultaneously: one against the Confederacy . . . and the other against a man who, like himself, wore blue," wrote Foote.

In their eagerness for results, executives frequently allow or even encourage internal competition. They say they want salespeople to work together, but what they want most is the sale, and if elbows fly in the process, so be it. Companies give lip service to partnerships and then create financial incentives for beating the other guy. The result is often a defeat for the organization caused by two generals spending as much time outmaneuvering each other as they do pursuing the objective.

Leaders working to unify their organizations often have their public relations staff create slogans aspiring to make their company "one." "One Company. One Team. One Passion," touts Coca-Cola. "One Company. One Team. One Goal," proclaims LexisNexis. "One Team, One Mission," states a U.S. Department of Homeland Security strategy document.

Without credible high-level commitments to following through, prominent partnership examples, the right incentives, and a truly collaborative culture, these slogans are just that — mere slogans. "It was obvious from the start that (our) sister company had a completely different culture than we did," reported one technology manager. "As software distributors, we shared many of the same product lines and dealt with many of the same technologies. We both did the same thing — sold tech products to computer retailers across the country and around the world. The merger failed miserably. We simply could not get along. There were too many egos and too many superstars. Eventually our West Coast outfit was closed in favor of the East Coast company."

Humans are naturally defensive and tribal. Their capacity for managing social networks is not great enough to encompass more than a couple hundred people, never mind all the people in "one" major corporation. Their opinions of the company are influenced most by their experiences within their own team, with their local manager, and with those in other departments with whom they share the smaller goals that feed into the company's larger mission. A collaboration between entities is nothing more than the sum of the individual partnerships between the two enterprises. Unless an organization's leaders attend to the details of those working relationships, the merger, the alliance, the joint marketing agreement, or whatever it's called, will certainly fail.

When Daimler-Benz AG merged with Chrysler in 1998, Daimler-Benz Chairman Jürgen Schrempp and Chrysler Chairman Robert Eaton appeared at an hour-long announcement event in neutral London heralding a "perfect fit of two leaders in their respective markets." They said it was a "merger of equals" and that the two of them would be co-chairmen. But the combination became more an acquisition of Chrysler than a merger, and despite some early victories, it didn't live up to its collaborative or financial billing.

"So far, DaimlerChrysler is a trans-Atlantic partnership mostly in name," observed the *International Herald Tribune* one year later. "DaimlerChrysler is pretty much run by Daimler executives. From the ubiquitous chief executive officer Jürgen Schrempp on down, the big decisions are made in Stuttgart. Chrysler managers complain they are lame ducks." Eaton left less than two years after the "merger of equals" press conference.

Nine years after the firms were combined on paper, Daimler left Chrysler by the side of the road for one-fifth of its original purchase price. "Chrysler was bought and was subsequently treated like a stepchild, not a partner," wrote one industry publication.

No leader who is a poor partner should expect to preside over a successful alliance between organizations. No leader who struggles to collaborate should expect his or her subordinate leaders or departments to do so. "Do what I say, not what I do" doesn't work any better here than it does in any other aspect of leadership.

One of the richest ironies in many organizations is that the executive urging partnerships on the managers and employees is someone who recently ousted his or her counterpart to take control of the combined enterprise. This spawns cascading Darwinian battles through operations, finance, sales, marketing, and every department where an executive sees more reason to compete than to cooperate.

Without powerful examples among the leaders, collaborations that began as a "merger of equals" degenerate into a series of cage matches that distract both camps from the business at hand. An enterprise that sets out to collaborate without building partnerships throughout will be worse off than one that never pretended to enter that dimension. Those partnerships begin at the top.

Appendix

How the Gallup Research
Was Conducted

★★

OVER THE PAST TWO DECADES, GALLUP has conducted exhaustive research on human nature and productivity in the workplace. Our research on collaboration grew from that larger body of discoveries.

Employee engagement is highly related to the positive relationships between supervisors and employees. It is well-established that a positive employee-supervisor collaborative relationship, rather than a hierarchical boss-underling relationship, is more conducive to employee engagement and subsequently to a more productive work environment. But what are the key elements of such well-functioning relationships? That was the research question that inspired this work.

From the research efforts outlined in this book emerged a theoretical model of what scholars sometimes call "dyadic collaborative relationships" in the workforce. The model was heavily influenced by a review of scholarly research on work partnerships, a thorough examination of the literature about each of the proposed elements of collaboration, and field studies completed by the authors and their colleagues.

The research can be classified into four broad categories:

1. Early work. In the late 1990s, informal, largely qualitative investigations were conducted. The investigators asked their colleagues and clients about supervisor-employee relationships and looked for patterns in their responses. They also conducted an extensive review of relevant literature. This latter effort yielded little with the exception of one key dissertation by Mary Leanna Ayers titled *Transformational Partnerships: A Relational Model of Dyadic Business Partnerships*. In her paper, Ayers proposes a model of the business partnership that "creates an environment in which each person in the relationship grows personally and professionally."

   Although little of the research addressed the elements of a successful partnership per se, the authors discovered a wealth of information about when and why people cooperate scattered in the scientific disciplines of behavioral economics, evolutionary psychology, primatology, neuroimaging, biology, computer science (Robert Axelrod's landmark tournaments), and traditional psychology. None of these data was sufficient alone, but when they were combined, a set of common themes presented itself.

In addition to the formal literature review, the investigators examined historical accounts of successful and failed partnerships, particularly those in which one partner or both left a first-person account of the collaboration. This investigation proved especially fruitful in understanding how the concepts from the various sciences play out in real-life conditions.

From this phase of investigation and brainstorming emerged a set of concepts and specific ideas about the difference between positive collaborative work relationships and those that were less productive. It became clear that the elements of a successful partnership were relatively consistent whether one was studying a partnership between work peers, between supervisor and employee, or between two people brought together to accomplish a goal outside of their employment.

2. Boss-partner studies. One of the most important issues for any workgroup is whether the manager of the team is perceived more as a boss or as a partner. Two extensive studies — one worldwide and the other in the United States — were conducted using a basic question: "Does your supervisor at work treat you more like he or she is your boss or your partner?"

In the worldwide study, more than 34,000 respondents in 108 countries were asked this question. All respondents had indicated that they were employed and had a supervisor at work. Worldwide, 53 percent said their supervisor treated them more like he or she was a partner.

There were clear differences by region. A higher percentage of people in the Americas and in Western Europe said that their supervisor treated them more like he or she was a partner compared to those in developed Asia (Japan, Korea, etc.) and former Soviet Union countries (Russia, et al.).

Treatment by Supervisor

Region	Sample Size	More like a boss	More like a partner	Don't know or refused
Total (worldwide)	34,323	41%	53%	6%
Latin America	5,644	35%	63%	2%
Western Europe, USA, Canada	7,523	35%	60%	4%
South Asia	2,777	37%	52%	11%
Central/East Central Europe	2,520	44%	49%	5%
Middle East/ Maghreb	3,634	47%	47%	6%
Sub-Saharan Africa	4,291	49%	47%	5%
Developed Asia	2,615	58%	37%	5%
Former Soviet Union Countries	5,319	62%	32%	5%

Worldwide, there were also clear differences in perceived quality of life measures between those whose supervisor treated them like he or she was a boss rather than a partner.

Treatment as a Partner by Supervisor Correlates With Quality of Life Measures — Worldwide Study (n=34,323)

My supervisor treats me more like he or she is	I am treated with respect all day	I am satisfied with my standard of living	I smiled/ laughed a lot
A boss	77%	61%	69%
A partner	86%	71%	77%

In the U.S.-only study, respondents were asked a similar set of questions, with similar results. In addition, in the United States, a subsample of respondents was asked to respond to Gallup's Q^{12} employee engagement items.

Treatment as a Partner by Supervisor Correlates With Quality of Life Measures — U.S. Study

My supervisor treats me more like he or she is	I am treated with respect all day (n=355,334)	I am satisfied with my standard of living (n=342,494)	I smiled/ laughed a lot (n=355,334)
A boss	86%	68%	80%
A partner	94%	78%	87%

Q^{12} Engagement and the
Boss-Partner Dichotomy — U.S. Study (n=5,577)

	My supervisor treats me more like he or she is	
	A boss	*A partner*
Actively disengaged	24%	4%
Not engaged	43%	35%
Engaged	33%	61%

From this set of studies, it is clear that those who consider their manager to be more like a partner than a boss have a more positive work environment. Managers who work as partners can anticipate higher performance from their teams; high levels of engagement correspond with higher customer scores, safety, retention, creativity, productivity, and profitability for the business.

3. Investigative studies. Using the hypotheses developed from the early work, a series of studies was conducted with random samples of U.S. residents using an Internet panel developed by Gallup. (More information about this panel is available below.)

Three studies were conducted:

a. March 2006: A sample of 796 employees who had a supervisor at work were asked a series of questions about their work life and about their supervisor relationships. They were also asked to evaluate that supervisor relationship.

b. March 2007: A sample of 100 people were asked to describe their best and worst partnerships using an open-ended question set. The respondents were asked to be as exhaustive as possible in their descriptions. A number of the anecdotes and quotes in this book come from these interviews.

c. September 2007: A random sample of 1,072 people from the general population were asked about their most positive, successful partnerships and also about less positive and less productive partnerships. At the time of the survey, 504 of the respondents were employees who had supervisors. These respondents were asked additional questions about their supervisor relationships.

4. Test construction study. From the three phases of investigative studies listed above, a set of scales was developed that clearly differentiated between good work partnerships and poor work partnerships. Those items were built around the theoretical model established from the early informal research, the literature reviews, and the first-person accounts of successful partnerships. The items were tested in the series of investigative research studies, and the best items were placed in the Gallup Partnership Rating Scales (GPRS). This instrument was then tested

more formally in a study of 1,086 people conducted via the Internet in December 2007. At the time of the survey, 621 of the respondents were employees who had supervisors. These respondents were asked additional questions about their supervisor relationships.

The Gallup Partnership Rating Scales

Through the research processes outlined above, an interview consisting of 21 items and 7 subscales was devised and tested. The following is a description of that instrument.

Several factor analyses of the items listed below (and other test items that were not included because of weak discriminating power) yielded a consistent set of three factors. These factors can be described as:

a. Complementary strengths

b. Common mission

c. Reciprocity

The best items in factors a and b were included in subtests that bear their names. The third factor (reciprocity) was dissected into five subtests:

c-1: Fairness

c-2: Trust

c-3: Acceptance

c-4: Communicating

c-5: Unselfishness

These subtests are highly intercorrelated, but they conceptually address five different aspects of reciprocity.

The actual scales are included below:*

Complementary Strengths:

- This person and I complement each other's strengths.

- This person and I need each other to get the job done.

- This person does some things much better than I do and I do some things much better than this person does.

Common Mission:

- This person and I share a common goal.

- This person and I have a common purpose for what we do.

- This person and I believe in the same mission in life.

Reciprocity:

Fairness:

- This person and I share the workload fairly between us.

- This person and I do not have to keep track of who does what and who gets credit for what.

- This person and I see each other as equals — one is not better than the other.

---

* The Gallup Partnership Rating Scales represent millions of dollars invested by Gallup researchers, and as such, they are proprietary. They cannot be reprinted or reproduced in any manner without the written consent of Gallup, Inc.

Trust:

- This person and I trust each other.

- This person and I can count on each other to do what the other says they will do.

- This person tells others how good I am and I tell them how good he or she is.

Acceptance:

- This person and I focus on each other's strengths, not weaknesses.

- This person and I accept each other as we are and do not try to change each other.

- This person and I are understanding of each other when one of us makes mistakes.

Communicating:

- Both this person and I rarely misunderstand each other.

- This person and I are good listeners for each other.

- This person and I show appreciation for what the other does.

Unselfishness:

- This person and I take as much satisfaction from seeing the other succeed as we do from our own success.

- This person is like a brother or sister to me.

- This person will risk a lot for me and I will do the same for him or her.

The authors' research on revenge and forgiveness led to the inclusion of two additional items that also discriminate well between strong and weak partnerships.

Forgiveness:

- There have been times when either this person or I have violated the other's trust.

- When either this person has or I have violated the other's trust, we have been able to forgive each other.

The Gallup Panel

For the data presented in this report, the GPRS was administered via the Internet to 1,086 randomly selected people who were members of the Gallup Panel.

The Gallup Panel was created in 2004 as a proprietary, probability-based longitudinal panel of U.S. households that have been selected using random digit dial (RDD) sampling methods. Panel households are recruited through an outbound phone interview, and they agree to participate in an average of three surveys per month via phone, Web, or mail. Once in the panel, members are not required to spend a specific predetermined amount of time as panelists. Rather, they are encouraged to remain members as long as they are willing and interested. There are no incentives or financial rewards for participating in the panel, though several token thank you gifts are sent throughout the year. Lastly, as with any longitudinal design, the Gallup Panel is affected by attrition. To leave the Gallup Panel, members can call the toll-free support phone number and request removal, or they are removed from the panel after they fail to respond to six consecutive surveys (with a postcard prompt after the third miss). Monthly attrition rate averages between 2 and 3 percent.

In addition to client-sponsored research, internal profile studies are conducted every three weeks with the entire adult panel population. These profile studies are designed to gather hundreds of behavioral, attitudinal, psychographic, and demographic statistics from the panelists. The data collected on these profile studies are used to target individuals for future custom research, to gain in-depth understanding of a particular industry or social issue, and to track longitudinal changes in panelist behavior and opinions.

The following chart shows the demographic characteristics of the sample for this study.

Comparison Sample for GPRS Study
(n=1,086)

	N	%
Gender:		
Male	512	47%
Female	562	52%
No response	12	1%
Age:		
Under 40	382	35%
40-54	410	38%
55 and older	284	26%
No response	10	1%

Comparison Sample for GPRS Study
(continued)

	N	%
Education:		
High school or less	196	18%
Some college	325	30%
College graduate	226	21%
Some postgraduate work	276	25%
No response	63	6%

Additional Technical Information

Each subtest in the Gallup Partnership Rating Scales has strong internal consistency (using appropriate Cronbach Alpha measures). Confirmatory factor analyses of each subtest determined that each was a single factor. The subtests are also intercorrelated.

The total score for the GPRS is highly discriminatory between "good partnerships" and "poor partnerships." In the test construction study (n=1,086), respondents were asked a series of other questions about the partnerships they rated and were also asked about their total workplace experience. Some of those findings are summarized below.

As noted earlier, each respondent was asked to rate a good partnership and a bad partnership. Respondents were then asked about the success of each partnership. The following chart summarizes these findings.

Judgments in accomplishing goals	Good partnerships	Poor partnerships
Judged as successful	98%	51%
Judged as unsuccessful	2%	49%
Accomplishment of the partnership		
Accomplished more than when alone	63%	33%
Accomplished less than when alone	26%	40%

By definition, the good partnerships were nearly all judged as successful, but even half of the poor partnerships were judged as successful in accomplishing their goals. It appears that a partnership can be seen as "successful" even if not all aspects of the relationship are clearly positive. In one-third of the poor partnerships, respondents said they accomplished more than they would have if they worked alone. Of course, the stronger partnerships were more likely to be successful than the poor partnerships. Yet even among good partnerships, 26 percent of respondents said they accomplished less working together than they would have alone. The evidence suggests that some missions do not require collaboration, and some individuals struggle to make partnerships, even strong partnerships, advantageous.

The GPRS and Work Engagement

The correlation between respondents' ratings of their partnership with their supervisor and their engagement at work is summarized in this section. Each person who rated his or her supervisor partnership was also asked to take the Gallup Q^{12}, a series of items developed to measure workplace engagement. Q^{12} results provide three categories of workplace engagement: engaged, not engaged, and actively disengaged. High levels of engagement correspond with higher customer scores, creativity, productivity, and profitability and lower levels of absenteeism, turnover, accidents, and inventory loss. The following chart shows the results of this comparison of 621 respondents who rated their supervisor partnerships.

GPRS level	Actively disengaged (n=99)*	Not engaged (n=320)*	Engaged (n=202)*
Very poor	10%	4%	9%
Poor	40%	19%	10%
Borderline	29%	22%	6%
Good	16%	35%	25%
Excellent	6%	20%	51%

*Numbers may not add up to 100% because of rounding.

From the results shown here, it is clear that the higher the GPRS level, the more likely the respondent is to be engaged and not actively disengaged. More than three-fourths (76 percent) of those who were engaged in their work rated their supervisor partnership in the good or excellent range. Conversely, most (79 percent) of those who were actively disengaged at work rated their supervisor partnership as borderline, poor, or very poor. Having a good partnership with one's supervisor is highly correlated with workplace engagement.

Final Comments

The Gallup Partnership Rating Scales (GPRS) is a research instrument and does not yet have the external validity or long-term use needed to be a diagnostic tool. However, through the thorough literature investigations, the investigative studies, and the creation of the Gallup Partnership Rating Scales, an interesting and actionable model emerged. Additional research using the GPRS will follow publication of this book.

Much is yet to be done. For example, although correlations between workplace engagement and workplace productivity have been established, no direct correlations are yet available between strong workplace partnerships and productivity. What has been accomplished, however, is a good starting place for future research and experimentation into the important relationship between two work collaborators.

Source Notes

★★

Gallup research was used extensively in writing this book. For complete details on that work, see the appendix: "How the Gallup Research Was Conducted."

INTRODUCTION: MADE FOR COLLABORATING

Cohen, Sheldon. "Social Relationships and Susceptibility to the Common Cold." *Emotion, Social Relationships, and Health.* Eds. Carol D. Ryff and Burton H. Singer. Oxford: Oxford UP, 2001. 221-242. Print.

de Castro, John M. "Eating Behavior: Lessons From the Real World of Humans." *Nutrition* 16.10 (2000): 800-813. Print.

Garrod, Simon, and Martin J. Pickering. "Why Is Conversation so Easy?" *Trends in Cognitive Sciences* 8.1 (2004): 8-11. Print.

Holt-Lunstad, Julianne, et. al. "Social Relationships and Ambulatory Blood Pressure: Structural and Qualitative Predictors of Cardiovascular Function During Everyday Social Interactions." *Health Psychology* 22.4 (2003): 388-397. Print.

House, James S., Karl R. Landis, and Debra Umberson. "Social Relationships and Health." *Science* 241.4865 (1988): 540-545. Print.

Huron, David. "Is Music an Evolutionary Adaptation?" *Annals of the New York Academy of Sciences* 930 (2001): 43-61. Print.

Johnson, Steven. "Emotions and the Brain." *Discover*. Discover, 1 April 2003. Web. 2 July 2009.

Karlgaard, Rich. "Real-World Advice for the Young." *Forbes* 11 April 2005: 41. Print.

Sebanz, Natalie. "It Takes Two to . . ." *Scientific American Mind* (2006-2007): 52-57. Print.

Sebanz, Natalie, Harold Bekkering, and Günther Knoblich. "Joint Action: Bodies and Minds Moving Together." *Trends in Cognitive Sciences* 10.2 (2006): 70-76. Print.

Wagner, Rodd, and James K. Harter. *12: The Elements of Great Managing*. New York: Gallup Press, 2006. Print.

Wilson, Gary. "How to Rein in the Imperial CEO." *The Wall Street Journal* 9 July 2008: A15. Print.

Wright, Robert. *The Moral Animal: Evolutionary Psychology and Everyday Life*. New York: Vintage Books, 1995. Print.

CHAPTER ONE: COMPLEMENTARY STRENGTHS

Ackman, Dan. "Disney, the Company vs. Disney, the Man." *Forbes.com*. Forbes, 10 Feb. 2007. Web. 28 June 2009.

"Aviation Accident Database & Synopses." NTSB Identification: SEA94FA096. *National Transportation Safety Board*. Web. 28 June 2009.

Cohen, Adam. *The Perfect Store: Inside eBay*. New York: Back Bay Books, 2003. Print.

Dunning, David, et. al. "Why People Fail to Recognize Their Own Incompetence." *Current Directions in Psychological Science* 12.3 (2003): 83-87. Print.

Eisner, Michael, and Tony Schwartz. *Work in Progress*. New York: Random House, 1998. Print.

Fabrikant, Geraldine. "Top Mouse: The Man Who Engineered the Disney Renaissance Tells His Own Story." Rev. of *Work in Progress*, by Michael Eisner and Tony Schwartz. *New York Times*. New York Times, 8 Nov. 1998. Web. 28 June 2009.

Gelb, Michael J. *How to Think Like Leonardo da Vinci: Seven Steps to Genius Every Day*. New York: Dell Publishing, 1998. Print.

The Holy Bible: King James Version. Peabody: Hendrickson, 2007. Print.

Kruger, Justin, and David Dunning. "Unskilled and Unaware of It: How Difficulties in Recognizing One's Own Incompetence Lead to Inflated Self-Assessments." *Journal of Personality and Social Psychology* 77.6 (1999): 1121-1134. Print.

Late Show with David Letterman. CBS. New York, 26 April 2007. Television.

Lewis, Michael C. Telephone interview. 6 July 2005.

Lowenstein, Roger. *Buffett: The Making of an American Capitalist*. New York: Random House, 1995. Print.

Luhm, Steve. "Johnny Be Good Hoops Bring Him Fame." *Salt Lake Tribune* 29 Jan. 1995: A1. Print.

Luhm, Steve. "No Bulls! Jazz Rally Back in Series." *The Salt Lake Tribune* 9 June 1997: B-1. Print.

Masters, Kim. "Deposed: The Strange Hiring and Firing of Michael Ovitz." *Slate.com*. The Washington Post, 16 Aug. 2004. Web. 28 June 2009.

Masters, Kim. *The Keys to the Kingdom: The Rise of Michael Eisner and the Fall of Everybody Else*. New York: HarperCollins, 2000. Print.

McCallum, Jack. "Big Wheel." *SI Vault*. Time Warner, 27 April 1992. Web. 23 June 2009.

McCallum, Jack. "Not a Passing Fancy." *SI Vault*. Time Warner, 25 April 1988. Web. 23 June 2009.

McCullough, David. *John Adams*. New York: Simon, 2001. Print.

Robbins, Anthony. *Awaken the Giant Within: How to Take Immediate Control of Your Mental, Emotional, Physical and Financial Destiny!* New York: Summit Books, 1991. Print.

Stewart, James B. *Disney War*. New York: Simon, 2005. Print.

Svenson, Ola. "Are We All Less Risky and More Skillful Than Our Fellow Drivers?" *Acta Psychologica* 47.2 (1981): 143-148. Print.

Taylor, Phil. "Pass Master." *SI Vault*. Time Warner, 16 June 1997. Web. 24 June 2009.

Wiley, Ralph. "Does He Ever Deliver!" *SI Vault*. Time Warner, 7 Nov. 1988. Web. 23 June 2009.

Zuckerman, Ezra W., and John T. Jost. "What Makes You Think You're So Popular? Self Evaluation Maintenance and the Subjective Side of the 'Friendship Paradox.'" *Social Psychology Quarterly* 64.3 (2001): 207-223. Print.

CHAPTER TWO: A COMMON MISSION

Bradford, Sarah H. *Documenting the American South*. "Scenes in the Life of Harriet Tubman: Electronic Edition." Web. 23 June 2009.

Hillary & Tenzing: Climbing to the Roof of the World. Dir. Margaret Percy. PBS DVD Video. 1996. DVD.

Hillary, Edmund. "The Conquest of the Summit." Comp. Beverley M. Bowie. *National Geographic* July 1954: 45-62. Print.

Hillary, Edmund. *High Adventure: The True Story of the First Ascent of Everest.* New York: Oxford UP, 2003. Print.

Humez, Jean M. "'*The Narrative of Sojourner Truth*' as a Collaborative Text." *Frontiers: A Journal of Women Studies* 16.1 (1996): 29-52. Print.

Mathieu, John E., et al. "The Influence of Shared Mental Models on Team Process and Performance." *Journal of Applied Psychology* 85.2 (2000): 273-283. Print.

Norgay, Tenzing, and James Ramsey Ullman. *Tiger of the Snows: The Autobiography of Tenzing of Everest.* New York: Putnam's, 1955. Print.

Painter, Nell Irvin. *Sojourner Truth: A Life, a Symbol.* Boston: Norton, 1997. Print.

Stewart, Jeffrey. Introduction. *Narrative of Sojourner Truth.* By Sojourner Truth. Oxford: Oxford UP, 1991. Print.

Truth, Sojourner, and Olive Gilbert. *Narrative of Sojourner Truth.* 1850. New York: Barnes & Noble, 2005. Print. The letter reproduced in this book was dictated by Sojourner Truth and addressed to Rowland Johnson, Nov. 17, 1864.

CHAPTER THREE: FAIRNESS

Amiel, Yoram, and Frank A. Cowell. *Thinking About Inequality: Personal Judgment and Income Distributions.* Cambridge: Cambridge UP, 2000. Print.

Brosnan, Sarah F., Cassiopeia Freeman, and Frans B.M. de Waal. "Partner's Behavior, Not Reward Distribution, Determines Success in an Unequal Cooperative Task in Capuchin Monkeys." *American Journal of Primatology* 68 (2006): 713-724. Print.

Brosnan, Sarah F., and Frans B.M. de Waal. "Monkeys Reject Unequal Pay." *Nature* 425. (2003): 297-299. Print.

Cohen, Adam. *The Perfect Store: Inside eBay*. New York: Back Bay Books, 2003. Print.

Drummond, Sara. "Multiplying Success." *Commercial Investment Real Estate*. CCIM Institute, Jan.-Feb. 2007. Web. 2 July 2009.

Hanna, Bill, and Tom Ito. *A Cast of Friends*. Cambridge: Da Capo, 2000. Print.

Hewlett, William. Interview by David Allison. "William Hewlett Oral History: Transcript of a Video History Interview With William Hewlett, Co-Founder, Hewlett Packard." 15 May 1995. Web. Transcript.

Howard, Fred. *Wilbur and Orville: A Biography of the Wright Brothers*. Mineola: Dover, 1998. Print.

Jacobellis v. Ohio. 378 US 184. Supreme Court of the US. 1964. *Supreme Court Collection*. Legal Information Inst., Cornell U Law School, n.d. Web. 3 July 2009.

Kruger, Justin, and Thomas Gilovich. "'Naïve Cynicism' in Everyday Theories of Responsibility Assessment: On Biased Assumptions of Bias." *Journal of Personality and Social Psychology* 76.5 (1999): 743-753. Print.

Malone, Michael S. *Bill & Dave: How Hewlett and Packard Built the World's Greatest Company*. New York: Portfolio, 2007. Print.

Packard, David. *The HP Way: How Bill Hewlett and I Built Our Company*. New York: Harper, 1995. Print.

Ross, Michael, and Fiore Sicoly. "Egocentric Biases in Availability and Attribution." *Journal of Personal and Social Psychology* 37.3 (1979): 322-336. Print.

Shackleton, Ernest H. *The Heart of the Antarctic*. Philadelphia: J. B. Lippencott, 1909. Print.

Van Praag, C. Mirjam, and Bernard M.S. van Praag. "The Benefits of Being Economics Professor A (and not Z)." IZA Discussion Papers 2673. Institute for the Study of Labor (IZA). Web. 3 July 2009.

CHAPTER FOUR: TRUST

"Antarctic Exploration." *History.com*. A&E Television Networks. 2009. Web. 14 July 2009.

Arnesen, Liv, and Ann Bancroft. *No Horizon is So Far: Two Women and Their Extraordinary Journey Across Antarctica*. Cambridge: Da Capo Press, 2003. Print.

Atlis, Mera M., et al. "Decision Processes and Interactions During a Two-Woman Traverse of Antarctica." *Environment and Behavior* 36.3. (2004): 402-423. Print.

Axelrod, Robert. *The Evolution of Cooperation*. New York: Basic, 2006. Print.

Bancroft Arnesen Explore. "Endurance." Bancroft Arnesen Explore. 2008. Web. 2 Aug. 2006.

Camerer, Colin F. *Behavioral Game Theory: Experiments in Strategic Interaction*. Princeton: Princeton UP, 2003. Print.

Fehr, Ernst, and Simon Gächter. "Fairness and Retaliation: The Economics of Reciprocity." *Journal of Economic Perspectives* 14 (2000): 159-181. Print.

Friend or Foe? Game Show Network, 2002-2003. Videocassette. Tapes from the research collection of John A. List, Ph.D., professor of economics, University of Chicago.

Hagenmeyer, S.J. "Albert W. Tucker, 89, Famed Mathematician." *Philadelphia Inquirer* Thursday, 2 Feb. 1995: B7. Print.

Hobbes, Thomas. *Leviathan: Or the Matter, Forme, and Power of a Commonwealth Ecclesiasticall and Civil.* 1651. New York: Touchstone, 2008. Print.

List, John A. *"Friend or Foe?* A Natural Experiment of the Prisoner's Dilemma." *Review of Economics & Statistics* 88.3 (2006): 463-471. Print.

Maas, Susan. "Prepped for the Trek." *Minnesota Medicine.* N.p. Nov. 2001. Web. 23 Feb. 2005.

Officer Gary. "Diary of Police Officer: Observations and Accounts of Life as a Police Officer." 25 Jan. 2006, 9:40 p.m. http://officergary.blogspot.com/2006/01/week-two-of-post-academy.html. Web. 3 July 2009.

Officer Gary. "Diary of Police Officer: Observations and Accounts of Life as a Police Officer." 21 June 2006, 9:29 p.m. http://officergary.blogspot.com/2006/06/busted.html. Web. 3 July 2009.

Poundstone, William. *Prisoner's Dilemma: John von Neumann, Game Theory and the Puzzle of the Bomb.* New York: Doubleday, 1993. Print.

Ridley, Matt. *The Origins of Virtue: Human Instincts and the Evolution of Cooperation.* New York: Penguin, 1998. Print.

CHAPTER FIVE: ACCEPTANCE

Andreoni, James, and Ragan Petrie. "Beauty, Gender and Stereotypes: Evidence from Laboratory Experiments." *Journal of Economic Psychology* 29:1 (2003): 73-93. Print.

Blalock, Alfred. *The Papers of Alfred Blalock.* Ed. Mark M. Ravitch. Baltimore: The Johns Hopkins Press, 1966. Print.

Brogan, Thomas V., and George M. Alfieris. "Has the Time Come to Rename the Blalock-Taussig Shunt?" *Pediatric Critical Care Medicine* 4.4 (2003): 450-453. Print.

DeBruine, Lisa M. "Facial Resemblance Enhances Trust." *Proceedings of the Royal Society of London B* 269 (2002): 1307-1312. Print.

Lewis, Michael. *To the Brink: Stockton, Malone, and the Utah Jazz's Climb to the Edge of Glory.* New York: Simon, 1998. Print.

Lewis, Michael C. Telephone interview. 6 July 2005.

McGehee, Harvey A. "Alfred Blalock." *Biographical Memoirs.* Office of the Home Secretary and National Academy of Sciences. Vol. 53. Washington, D.C.: National Academy, 1982. 49-82. Print.

McPherson, Miller, Lynn Smith-Lovin, and James M. Cook. "Birds of a Feather: Homophily in Social Networks." *Annual Review of Sociology* 27 (2001): 415-44. Print.

Murphy, Warren. "Writing With a Partner, or . . . What Part of 'No' Don't You Understand." Ed. Sue Grafton. *Writing Mysteries: A Handbook by the Mystery Writers of America.* Cincinnati: Writer's Digest, 2002. 26-32. Print.

Nakamura, Yuka Maya, and Ulrich Orth. "Acceptance as a Coping Reaction: Adaptive or Not?" *Swiss Journal of Psychology* 64.4 (2005): 281-292. Print.

Partners of the Heart. Dir. Andrea Kalin and Bill Duke. Prod. WGBH. PBS: American Experience, 2003. Film.

Paul, Richard W., and Linda Elder. *Critical Thinking: Tools for Taking Charge of Your Professional and Personal Life.* Upper Saddle River: Financial Times Prentice Hall, 2002. Print.

Roy, Michael M., and Nicholas J.S. Christenfeld. "Do Dogs Resemble Their Owners?" *Psychological Science* 15.5 (2004): 361-363. Print.

Segal, Nancy L., and Scott L. Hershberger. "Cooperation and Competition Between Twins: Findings from a Prisoner's Dilemma Game." *Evolution and Human Behavior* 20 (1999): 29-51. Print.

Thomas, Vivien. *Partners of the Heart: Vivien Thomas and His Work with Alfred Blalock*. Philadelphia: U of Pennsylvania P, 1985. Print.

CHAPTER SIX: FORGIVENESS

Adams, John. "To Thomas Jefferson" 1 Jan. 1811. Letter. Ed. Lester J. Cappon. *The Adams-Jefferson Letters: The Complete Correspondence Between Thomas Jefferson and Abigail and John Adams*. Chapel Hill: U of North Carolina P, 1987. Print.

Breuer, Joseph, and Sigmund Freud. 1895. *Studies in Hysteria*. N.p.: Karig, 2007. Print.

Bushman, Brad J. "Does Venting Anger Feed or Extinguish the Flame? Catharsis, Rumination, Distraction, Anger, and Aggressive Responding." *Personality and Social Psychology Bulletin* 28.6 (2002): 724-731. Print.

Chambers, Timothy. "Readers Report: Revenge in Business: Handle With Care." Message to *BusinessWeek*. 12 Feb. 2007. Letter.

de Quervain, Dominique J.-F., et al. "The Neural Basis of Altruistic Punishment." *Science* 305:5688 (2004): 1254-1258. Print.

Ellis, Joseph J. *Founding Brothers: The Revolutionary Generation*. New York: Knopf, 2000. Print.

Grover, Ronald. "How Eisner Saved the Magic Kingdom." *BusinessWeek*. McGraw-Hill, 30 Sept. 2005. Web. 6 July 2009.

Hayden, Thomas. "Why We Need Nosy Parkers." *U.S. News & World Report*. U.S. News & World Report, 5 June 2005. Web. 5 July 2009.

Hornberger, R.H. "The Differential Reduction of Aggressive Responses as a Function of Interpolated Activities." *American Psychologist* 14 (1959): 354. Print.

"Interview: Jeffrey Katzenberg, DreamWorks Founder and Shrek Producer." Film. *The Independent*. Independent News and Media Limited, 22 June 2007. Web. 16 July 2009.

Jacoby, Susan. *Wild Justice: The Evolution of Revenge*. New York: Harper, 1983. Print.

Jefferson, Thomas. "To John Adams." 21 Jan. 1812. Letter. Ed. Lester J. Cappon. *The Adams-Jefferson Letters: The Complete Correspondence Between Thomas Jefferson and Abigail and John Adams*. Chapel Hill: U of North Carolina P, 1987. Print.

Jefferson, Thomas. "To John Adams." 27 June 1813. Letter. Ed. Lester J. Cappon. *The Adams-Jefferson Letters: The Complete Correspondence Between Thomas Jefferson and Abigail and John Adams*. Chapel Hill: U of North Carolina P, 1987. Print.

Lee, John. *Facing the Fire: Experiencing and Expressing Anger Appropriately*. New York: Bantam, 1993. Print.

McCullough, David. *John Adams*. New York: Simon, 2001. Print.

McCullough, Michael E., Lindsey M. Root, and Adam D. Cohen. "Writing About the Benefits of an Interpersonal Transgression Facilitates Forgiveness." *Journal of Consulting and Clinical Psychology* 74.5 (2006): 887-897. Print.

McGregor, Jena. "Sweet Revenge." *BusinessWeek*. McGraw-Hill, 22 Jan. 2007. Web. 5 July 2009.

Mitgang, Herbert. "Books of the Times; After War, Coming Home to an Uneasy Life." *New York Times*. New York Times, 3 Feb. 1990. Web. 5 July 2009.

Persico, Joseph E. *Edward R. Murrow: An American Original*. New York: McGraw-Hill, 1988. Print.

Quincy, Josiah. *Figures of the Past: From the Leaves of Old Journals*. Boston: Roberts, 1883. *Google Book Search*. Web. 7 July 2009.

Rich, Laura. "Mickey Mouse's Worst Nightmare." *The Industry Standard*. The Industry Standard, 14 May 2001. Web. 6 July 2009.

Shirer, William L. *Berlin Diary: The Journal of a Foreign Correspondent, 1934-1941*. Baltimore: Johns Hopkins UP, 2002. Print.

"A Thousand Tiny Cuts: Life's Small Annoyances." *Talk of the Nation*. Natl. Public Radio, 31 March 2005. Radio.

Tripp, Thomas M., Robert J. Bies, and Karl Aquino. "Poetic Justice or Petty Jealousy? The Aesthetics of Revenge." *Organizational Behavior and Human Decision Processes* 89 (2002): 966-984. Print.

CHAPTER SEVEN: COMMUNICATING

Brosig, Jeannette. "Identifying Cooperative Behavior: Some Experimental Results in a Prisoner's Dilemma Game." *Journal of Economic Behavior & Organization* 47.3 (2002): 275-290. Print.

Carlos, et al. "The Effect of Communication Modality on Cooperation in Online Environments." *Microsoft Research*. Technical Report MSR-TR-99-75. (1999). Print.

"Collision With Trees and Crash Short of the Runway, Corporate Airlines Flight 5966, BAE Systems BAE-J3201, N875JX, Kirksville, Missouri, October 19, 2004." Aircraft Accident Report: NTSB/AAR-06/01. *National Transportation Safety Board.* Web. 7 July 2009.

Corballis, Michael. "The Uniqueness of Human Recursive Thinking." *American Scientist* (2007): 240-248. Print.

Crick, Francis. *What Mad Pursuit: A Personal View of Scientific Discovery.* New York: Basic Books, 1990. Print.

Fouracre, Ronald, and Peter Shaw. "A Triumph of 'Brain Work' and Good Fortune." Video Clips. *The Race for DNA: A Documentary History.* Wiley, 1973. Web. 8 July 2009.

Kirkpatrick, David, et al. "Dell and Rollins: The $41 Billion Buddy Act." *Fortune* April 2004: 84. Print.

Maddox, Brenda. *Rosalind Franklin: The Dark Lady of DNA.* New York: HarperCollins, 2003. Print.

Manzini, Paola, Abdolkarim Sadrieh, and Nicolass J. Vriend. "On Smiles, Winks, and Handshakes as Coordination Devices." *The Economic Journal* 119.537 (2009): 826-854. Print.

Nova Scotia (Human Rights Commission) v. Play It Again Sports Ltd. NSCA 132 No. 403. Nova Scotia Court of Appeal. 2004. Print.

Povinelli, Daniel J., and Jennifer Vonk. "Chimpanzee Minds: Suspiciously Human?" *Trends in Cognitive Sciences* 7.4 (2003): 157-160. Print.

Ridley, Matt. *Francis Crick: Discoverer of the Genetic Code.* New York: HarperCollins, 2006. Print.

Roosevelt, Theodore. *Through the Brazilian Wilderness.* 1914. Lanham: Cooper Square, 2000. Print.

Scharlemann, Jörn P.W., et al. "The Value of a Smile: Game Theory With a Human Face." *Journal of Economic Psychology* 22.5 (2001): 617-640. Print.

Sheldon, Kennon M. "Learning the Lessons of Tit-for-Tat: Even Competitors Can Get the Message." *Journal of Personality and Social Psychology* 77.6 (1999): 1245-1253. Print.

Watson, James D. *Double Helix: A Personal Account of the Discovery of the Structure of DNA*. New York: Scribner, 1998. Print.

Watson, James D., and F.H.C. Crick. "A Structure for Deoxyribose Nucleic Acid." *Nature* 171.4356 (1953): 737-738. Print.

Wilkins, Maurice. *The Third Man of the Double Helix: The Autobiography of Maurice Wilkins*. Oxford: Oxford UP, 2003. Print.

Wright, Robert. "James Watson & Francis Crick." *Time* 100. *Time*. Time, 29 March 1999. Web. 8 July 2009.

CHAPTER EIGHT: UNSELFISHNESS

Alexander, Caroline. *Endurance: Shackleton's Legendary Antarctic Expedition*. New York: Knopf, 1998. Print.

Cauldwell, K. "The Science of Altruism? Researchers Discover Brain Patterns Associated With Selflessness." *Associated Content*. 31 Jan. 2007. Web. 10 July 2009.

Darwin, Charles. *The Descent of Man*. 1879. London: Penguin, 2004. Print.

Dawkins, Richard. *The Selfish Gene*. 1976. New York: Oxford UP, 1990. Print.

Fehr, Ernst, and Suzann-Viola Renninger. "The Samaritan Paradox." *Scientific American Mind* (2004): 15-21. Print.

Franklin, Benjamin, William Temple Franklin, and William Duane. *Memoirs of Benjamin Franklin*. Philadelphia: M'Carty & Davis, 1834. *Google Book Search*. Web. 10 July 2009.

Freeman, Karen. "Amos Tversky, Expert on Decision Making, Is Dead at 59" *New York Times*. New York Times, 6 June 1996. Web. 13 July 2009.

Kahneman, Daniel, and Amos Tversky. "Prospect Theory: An Analysis of Decision Under Risk." *Econometrica* 47.2 (1979): 263-292. Print.

Les Prix Nobel. "The Nobel Prizes 2002." Ed. Tore Frängsmyr. Stockholm: Nobel Foundation, 2003. Print.

Mill, Hugh Robert. *The Life of Sir Ernest Shackleton*. Whitefish: Kessinger, 2006. Print.

Moll, Jorge, et al. "The Neural Basis of Human Moral Cognition." *Nature Reviews: Neuroscience* 6 (2005): 799-809. Print.

Moll, Jorge, et al. "The Neural Correlates of Moral Sensitivity: A Functional Magnetic Resonance Imaging Investigation of Basic and Moral Emotions." *The Journal of Neuroscience* 22.7 (2002): 2730-2736. Print.

Morrell, Margot. Message to Rodd Wagner. 12 March 2005. E-mail.

Riffenburgh, Beau. *Shackleton's Forgotten Expedition: The Voyage of the Nimrod*. New York: Bloomsbury, 2004. Print.

Singer, Tania, et al. "Brain Responses to the Acquired Moral Status of Faces." *Neuron* 41.4 (2004): 653-662. Print.

Tankersley, Dharol, Jill Stowe, and Scott A. Huettel. "Altruism Is Associated With an Increased Neural Response to Agency." *Nature Neuroscience* 10.2 (2007): 150-151. Print.

Tversky, Amos, and Daniel Kahneman. "Judgment Under Uncertainty: Heuristics and Biases." *Science* 185.4157 (1974): 1124-1131. Print.

Tversky, Amos, and Daniel Kahneman. "Rational Choice and the Framing of Decisions." Part 2: The Behavioral Foundations of Economic Theory. *The Journal of Business* 59.4 (1986): S251-S278. Print.

FOR MANAGERS: A BOSS OR A PARTNER?

Fehr, Ernst, and Simon Gächter. "Do Incentive Contracts Undermine Voluntary Cooperation?" Working Paper No. 34. *Institute for Empirical Research in Economics*. Switzerland: University of Zurich, 2000. Print.

Wagner, Rodd, and James K. Harter. *12: The Elements of Great Managing*. New York: Gallup Press, 2006. Print.

FOR LEADERS: CREATING COLLABORATIVE ORGANIZATIONS

Andrews, Edmund L., and Laura M. Holson. "Shaping a Global Giant." *New York Times* 7 May 1998, sec A:1. Print.

Buono, Anthony F., and James L. Bowditch. *The Human Side of Mergers and Acquisitions: Managing Collisions Between People, Cultures, and Organizations*. Frederick: Beard, 2003. Print.

Fitzpatrick, Dan. "Soaring Stock Prices Suggest Better Days Are Ahead for Airlines." *Pittsburgh Post-Gazette*. Pittsburgh Post-Gazette. 8 Dec. 2005. Web. 14 July 2009.

Foote, Shelby. *The Beleaguered City: The Vicksburg Campaign, December 1862-July 1863*. New York: Modern Library, 1995. Print.

Hayward, Tony. "How Do We Deliver Energy for Sustainable Growth?" World Petroleum Council, Madrid, Spain. 30 June 2008. Speech.

Krebs, Michelle. "Daimler-Chrysler: Why the Marriage Failed." *Edmunds AutoObserver*. Edmunds Automotive Network, 17 May 2007. Web. 15 July 2009.

Krug, Jeffrey A., and Walt Shill. "The Big Exit: Executive Churn in the Wake of M&As." *Journal of Business Strategy* 29.4 (2008): 15-21. Print.

Malone, Tim. "IT Involvement in Mergers and Acquisitions." *TechRepublic*. CBS Interactive, 19 March 2008. Web. 15 July 2009.

"Market Profile - December 17, 2001." *AllBusiness.com*. Dun & Bradstreet, 17 Dec. 2001. Web. 14 July 2009.

Morton, John. "Blood Ties Drive A Deal." *American Journalism Review*. University of Maryland Foundation, November 1998. Web 14 July 2009.

Revah, Suzan. "Bylines." *American Journalism Review*. University of Maryland Foundation, December 1996. Web. 14 July 2009.

Romenesko, Jim. "Memos Sent to Romenesko: NYT Newsroom Integration Memo." *Poynter Online*. The Poynter Institute, 2 Aug. 2005. Web. 14 July 2009.

"Sinclair to Buy 6 Guy Gannett TV Stations." *New York Times*. New York Times, 10 Sept. 1998. Web. 14 July 2009.

Sullivan, Aline. "For Trailblazing DaimlerChrysler, a Rocky Road to Globalization." *International Herald Tribune* 18 Sept. 1999, Money Report sec.: 15. Print.

Toner, Mark. "Profile: Guy Gannett Communications." *Presstime*. Newspaper Association of America, January 1998. Web. 14 July 2009.

United States. Office of the Director of National Intelligence. *Vision 2015: A Globally Networked and Integrated Intelligence Enterprise.* Washington, D.C. 2009. Print.

Ureneck, Lou. *Backcast: Fatherhood, Fly-fishing, and a River Journey Through the Heart of Alaska.* New York: St. Martin's, 2007. Print.

Wagner, Rodd, and James K. Harter. *12: The Elements of Great Managing.* New York: Gallup Press, 2006. Print.

Wilson, Rob. "Daimler-Chrysler Merger Should Be Dynamite Combination If It Just Follows the Successful Daimler Freightliner Pattern." *Diesel Progress North American Edition* 1 June 1998. Print.

APPENDIX: HOW THE GALLUP RESEARCH WAS CONDUCTED

Ayers, Mary Leanna. *Transformational Partnerships: A Relational Model of Dyadic Business Partnerships.* Diss. Fielding Graduate Institute, 2002. Ann Arbor: UMI, 2003. Print.

Wagner, Rodd, and James K. Harter. *12: The Elements of Great Managing.* New York: Gallup Press, 2006. Print.

Acknowledgements

THIS BOOK IS THE RESULT of more than the partnership between the two of us. Many collaborators brought their unique strengths to bear, and we are indebted to each of them.

Editor Geoff Brewer was, at turns, our advocate, critic, and counselor. He was the perfect combination of patience, insistence, and flexibility through a writing process that was unavoidably tumultuous because we were uniting many disparate sciences and stories. His observations were directly on point, and if we briefly balked at certain rewrites, cuts, and rearranging, it was only because we knew he was right. This book is as much his as it is ours.

Executive Publisher Larry Emond was simultaneously supportive and skeptical, both of which served the goal of getting from us the best book from our research. We muttered and grumbled along the way. Now we are grateful. Associate Publisher Dr. Piotr J. Juszkiewicz once again flawlessly managed all of the operations, from cover design to marketing and promotion to getting the presses rolling. He too gave us helpful and thoughtful editorial suggestions.

Trista Kunce was intensely vigilant with her verification of facts and sources, causing us eventually to question whether the sun in fact rises in the east. Kelly Henry brought a rare combination of insight and thoroughness on deadline to the book's final preparations for print. Barb Sanford helped develop much of our material into compelling articles for the *Gallup Management Journal*. They were led by their superb manager, Kelly Slater. Chin-Yee Lai's cover and Samantha Allemang's interior design are wonderful icing on the cake. Alyssa Yell was a sounding board and advisor for several stylistic issues. Joy Murphy helped manage the production process for this book. Barbara Cave Henricks and Sara Schneider proved once again to be world-class publicists.

Rachel Brown and Heather Totin tracked down much of the secondary research, some of it tucked in quite obscure corners. They were both incredible detectives over many months. Paula Wilhelm's air traffic control work during the culminating months was instrumental in getting it off to the presses, as was the ongoing typing and coordinating efforts of Linda Bjorkman and Rachel Penrod.

When, after repeated attempts, we could not get so much as a simple reply from the Game Show Network, University of Chicago Economics Professor John A. List was kind enough to loan us the tapes of *Friend or Foe?* he used for his research. We consider Dr. List a friend. The Game Show Network is our foe (but we are working on forgiving them).

Salt Lake Tribune sports reporters Michael C. Lewis and Phil Miller provided crucial insights into the partnership between Utah Jazz players John Stockton and Karl Malone. Margot Morrell, coauthor of *Shackleton's Way*, was very willing to share notes and observations from her original research on the relationship between Ernest Shackleton and Frank Wild. Steve Ruedisili gave us a first-edition copy of Tenzing Norgay's autobiography, *Tiger of the Snows*, which led us to include the quintessential partnership of Tenzing and Edmund Hillary.

Battalion Chief Charles Hermann of the Rochester, Minnesota, Fire Department — Rodd's best friend in the seventh grade — checked his memory and the chemistry of the oxygen-acetylene balloon incident from their shared days in junior high shop class. During a November 2007 flight delay, Northwest Airlines Captain Mark Schwinge invited passengers to visit the flight deck. Beating out a line of 5-year-olds and their mothers, Rodd was invited to sit in the first officer's seat by Captain Schwinge, who agreed to an impromptu interview and subsequently sent a page of eloquent thoughts on collaboration in the cockpit.

Many colleagues, friends, and subscribers to the *Gallup Management Journal* read the manuscript and offered their insights. Among them were Russ Ackerman, Jim Asplund, Dr. Paul Bruer, Jon Clifton, Mike Danielski, Brett Elmendorf, Cynthia English, Dr. Larry Firkins, Steve Grizzell, Paul Haik, Dr. James K. Harter, Quentin Hill, Dr. Brent J. Johnson, Steve Loheit, Gregg Murray, Chad

Peel, Scott Perkins, Eldon Richards, Pete Starren, Amanda Wrangham, and Paula Wilhelm. We hope we have done justice to their recommendations.

Dr. Glenn Phelps and Eric Olesen played crucial roles in analyzing Gallup's research to identify the best statements to measure the strength of a partnership.

In memory, we thank Dr. Donald O. Clifton, who was the ultimate partner to many and whose ideas are central to our theoretical framework.

Many of the ideas for the book were inspired by Gale's experiences over many years as a partner and manager. We would be remiss in not mentioning some of those key work partnerships. Early in his career, successful partnerships included those with Gene Carroll, Mercedes Crawford, Alfredo Gamez, Luis Guzman, Larry Johnson, Connie Rath, Vic Resendez, Ted Rethmeier, and Mike Wortman. At Gallup, in addition to those already mentioned above, some of the most successful partnerships included those with Scott Ahlstrand, Dave Bauer, Dr. Cheryl Beamer, Jeff Bechtolt, Patrick Bogart, Richard Burkholder, Hess Dyas, Sherry Erhlich, Neli Esipova, Johanna Godoy, Agnes Illyes, Chris McCarty, Jan Miller, JoAnn Miller, Lymari Morales, Matt Mosser, Dr. Frank Newport, Nicole Naurath, Dr. Susan Nugent, Steve O'Brien, Dr. Anita Pugliese, Julie Ray, Jesus Rios, Phil Ruhlman, CK Sharma, Linda Slovic, Dr. Rajesh Srinivasan, Annette Templeton, Dr. Bob Tortora, Dr. Mary Trouba, John Wood, and Dr. Tao Wu.

Some of the best models of great partnership are Gallup's top executives: Jim Krieger, CFO; Jane Miller, COO; and Jim Clifton, Chairman and CEO. For Gale, each has been a best friend at work and a work partner who made life better and made work fun and highly productive.

This book was substantially influenced by the example of Dr. John Dykes, fellow scoutmaster with Rodd of Boy Scout Troop 3295, Northern Star Council, during much of the writing. Scoutmaster Dykes epitomized each of the eight elements of partnership under the pressure of ensuring the safety and progress of a dozen scouts through ax handling, fire building, sudden thunderstorms, and the coordinated attack on camp of a small army of raccoons.

Gale is especially appreciative of the lifelong influence of his family. His brothers, Gary, Denny, and Dean, and his sister, Kathy, and their spouses and families have been a great source of strength. Gale's parents were a model partnership in life and in business, and early in life, his Aunt Shirley always treated him as an "equal adult." A special thank you goes to Gale's good friend and son, Ed, and Ed's wonderful wife, Leigh Ann, and their very special children, Atticus, Helena, Henson, and Dasha. Thank you to his daughter, Kelly, who always brings joy into lives and to her life partner, Josh, who has been her perfect complement. And, most of all, Gale thanks Kay for being his perfect partner and for making him a whole person.

Rodd's wife, Nora, and their children, Noelle, Parks, and Charlie made innumerable sacrifices to allow the book to be completed. Noelle, your enthusiasm to read the manuscript was hugely encouraging. Thank you, Parks, for being a perfectly trustworthy climbing and scuba partner. Thank you, Charlie, for cheering me on through several of the toughest rewriting days. And thank you, Nora, for a thousand gentle course corrections. *Power of 2* could not have been written without their understanding and support.

As coauthors of a book about partnership, we endeavored to follow our own advice. We think we did fairly well. We certainly had a great time making these discoveries together, and we accomplished something neither of us could have done by himself. We got a nice souvenir of our collaboration. It is deeply rewarding to know that long after we both have passed away, somewhere on some bookshelf we will be known as partners.

About the Authors

RODD WAGNER is a *New York Times* bestselling author and a principal of Gallup. His books, speeches, and consulting focus on how human nature affects business strategy. He advises senior executives in numerous industries on the best ways to strengthen their partnerships, increase employee engagement, and improve profitability. Wagner and James K. Harter, Ph.D., are authors of *12: The Elements of Great Managing*, an American and Canadian bestseller published in 10 languages.

Wagner holds an M.B.A. with honors from the University of Utah Graduate School of Business. He was formerly the research director of the *Portland Press Herald* in Maine, a reporter and news editor for *The Salt Lake Tribune*, and a radio talk show host. When not writing or consulting, Wagner enjoys fly-fishing, snowboarding, and coaching youth lacrosse. He, his wife, Nora, and their children Noelle, Parks, and Charlie live near Minneapolis.

GALE MULLER is vice chairman and general manager of the Gallup World Poll. As the project leader for the World Poll, Muller oversees a global team of researchers who study and report on the voices of citizens in more than 150 countries and areas. This endeavor represents one of the largest research programs in the world and includes topics such as well-being, Muslim-West relations, poverty, and economic development.

Muller joined Gallup in 1973. From 1975 to 1979, he was a member and later general manager of SRI Perceiver Academies — then the company's educational consulting and training division. He served as director of operations for Gallup's survey research center from 1979 until 1984. As director of analysis from 1984 to 2005, Muller was a primary consultant and developed research-based marketing plans and growth strategies for many of Gallup's major accounts.

During his 35-plus years at Gallup, Muller ran a network of more than 300 consultants and researchers who were located in more than 40 cities throughout the world. He has developed multiple selection instruments and engineered their deployment in organizations around the world, and he developed research-based strategies for growth for dozens of organizations. Throughout his career, he has worked on many of Gallup's key client accounts in the automotive, entertainment, telecommunications, healthcare, and broadcast industries.

Muller received his bachelor's degree in mathematics and his master's and doctoral degrees in educational psychology and measurements from the University of Nebraska-Lincoln. He currently serves on the boards of a number of non-profit organizations in the Omaha-Lincoln area. Muller and his wife, Kay, have two children, Ed and Kelly, and four grandchildren, Atticus, Helena, Henson, and Dasha.

Gallup Press exists to educate and inform the people who govern, manage, teach, and lead the world's six billion citizens. Each book meets Gallup's requirements of integrity, trust, and independence and is based on Gallup-approved science and research.